iDENTIFICATION GUIDES

British Birds

Publisher and Creative Director: Nick Wells
Project Editor: Sara Robson
Picture Research: Gemma Walters
Consultant Naturalist: Chris McLaren
Art Director: Mike Spender
Digital Design and Production: Chris Herbert
Layout Design: Basil UK Ltd.

Special thanks to: Victoria Garrard, Julie Pallot, Sarah Sherman and Claire Walker

12 14 16 15 13
9 10

This edition first published 2007 by
FLAME TREE PUBLISHING
Crabtree Hall, Crabtree Lane
Fulham, London SW6 6TY
United Kingdom
www.flametreepublishing.com

Flame Tree Publishing is part of the Foundry Creative Media Co. Ltd.

© 2007 text and artwork illustrations A. Pearson and M. Lambert
© 2007 in the original edition Malcolm Saunders Publishing Ltd.
This edition produced under a licence granted by Malcolm Saunders Publishing Ltd.

© 2007 this edition The Foundry Creative Media Co. Ltd.

ISBN 978-1-84451-839-5

A CIP record for this book is available from the British Library upon request.

All photographs courtesy of Corbis.

Printed in China

IDENTIFICATION GUIDES

British Birds

Mike Lambert and Alan Pearson

FLAME TREE
PUBLISHING

Contents

Introduction

The chief aim of this book is to enable the reader, and newcomer to birdwatching, to identify positively and as simply as possible the great majority of birds which he is likely to encounter.

We all come into contact with birds, most of us with more interest and curiosity than specialist knowledge. This simple guide will enable you to identify a bird seen on a country walk, on holiday, or a visitor to the back garden, and will add to the casual observer's knowledge of common bird species.

There is, to be sure, no shortage of books on birds, but most of them group birds in families which makes identification a confusing and time-consuming process. A bird is unlikely to wait around and pose helpfully while the enthusiastic beginner leafs through an entire list of birds in the hope of identifying the species before him. If he has little or no idea which family a particular bird might belong to, where is he to begin?

Similarly, it is often difficult to establish from traditional guides whether a bird is a real rarity or merely a little uncommon. Thus it would be a simple error to decide that a small thin-billed greenish little bird was a Greenish Warbler, when it was in fact the far more common Willow Warbler.

Identification Guide: British Birds avoids confusion by editing out rarities such as the Greenish Warbler. Only the most common species have been featured and it is worth stressing that these are not necessarily the most common in terms of numbers, but those that the non-expert beginner is most likely to meet. So birds that are shy of humans or that are found only in inaccessible regions have been omitted, since they are only rarely seen. So you will not have to go out of your way to see any of the birds featured here and with the help of this simple identification guide you will, we hope, increase and expand your interest and knowledge.

Most of the more unusual species are listed in group colour plates in the **Less Common Species section** (pp. 332–47). If you regularly see species from this additional selection, then you have probably outgrown this book and should seek more specialist guides.

How to Use this Book

To enable the newcomer to birdwatching to make a positive identification as simply as possible, we have divided the birds into sections according to the type of location where you are most likely to see them. If, for instance, you want to identify a bird seen on a walk in the woods, you should consult the **Birds of Town, Garden, Park and Woodland** section.

Within each of the sections, birds are not ordered by family but by size, since it is grouping by family that makes most bird guides so difficult for beginners to follow. So, knowing where you saw the bird and having turned to the appropriate section, you need to make a rough guess at its size.

How Big was the Bird?

Birds are featured in order of size from smallest to largest and the relative size category is denoted by a symbol at the top of each page beside the name of the bird (see Fig. 1). This means that two birds of the same family may be separated by a bird or birds of intermediate size. For example, two of the commonest Woodpeckers will be found as follows: Great Spotted at 23 cm (9 in) and Green Woodpecker at 32 cm (12–13 in).

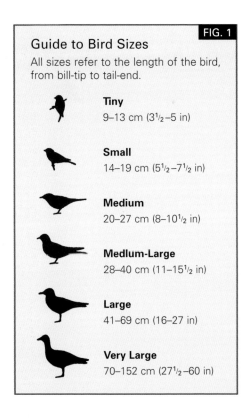

FIG. 1

Guide to Bird Sizes

All sizes refer to the length of the bird, from bill-tip to tail-end.

Tiny
9–13 cm (3$\frac{1}{2}$–5 in)

Small
14–19 cm (5$\frac{1}{2}$–7$\frac{1}{2}$ in)

Medium
20–27 cm (8–10$\frac{1}{2}$ in)

Medium-Large
28–40 cm (11–15$\frac{1}{2}$ in)

Large
41–69 cm (16–27 in)

Very Large
70–152 cm (27$\frac{1}{2}$–60 in)

By flicking through the book you have quickly narrowed the field down to birds of a particular size in a particular location. The information you need to make a positive identification is contained on the left-hand page beside the illustration of each bird. A specimen spread is shown in Fig. 2 (on p.13).

Distinguishing Marks

The first paragraph, under **Primary Features**, describes the feature or combination of features that are unique to that bird of that size range. In other words, if you are certain of these features, which are also borne out by the colour illustration, you have already *positively identified* the bird and need read on only out of interest and to build up a more detailed picture of it.

If you are uncertain about these specific features, then the **Secondary Features** paragraph completes the description. The third paragraph adds localities and typical habits. However, **Secondary Features** and **Localities, Habits and Song**, although they provide additional information, do not specifically identify the particular bird. Only the **Primary Features** paragraphs can do that.

The last paragraph on each entry gives the names of similar birds with which the featured bird could be confused. All these 'lookalikes' are either featured in detail themselves or appear under the heading of **Less Common Species**. The names and features of less common birds are given in brackets, so if you turn to page 104, *Collared Dove*, you will see its lookalikes listed as *(Turtle Dove:...)* *Feral Pigeon* and *Wood Pigeon*. This means that the Feral and Wood Pigeon are featured in the first three sections, while the Turtle Dove is to be found under **Less Common Species**.

Lookalikes

The **Lookalikes** paragraph is important for two reasons. Firstly it is all too easy to jump to conclusions when looking for known identifying features. You can, in effect, already have made up your mind about the bird's identify before checking its specific features in the first paragraph. Check the **Lookalikes** carefully. Size is easily misjudged and buff plumage, for instance, often mistaken for yellow. This paragraph will give you other possibilities to consider.

Secondly, it is very important for the observer to be aware of exactly what points he should be looking for, as a means of quickly distinguishing similar birds. This is where guesswork ends and skill begins.

After the three sections of birds featured individually according to typical habitat, the last section is a grouping, again in strictly size order, of other species which are likely to be observed by non-experts. No text accompanies the illustrations, just the name and size of each species, with its distinguishing features pinpointed.

Before you set out, it is worth emphasising that birds are not glued to their habitat and may travel widely. The habitat divisions in this book indicate the most likely location for each bird. But be prepared to consider information in **Localities, Habits and Song** if you feel sure that you have seen a bird out of habitat. Any usual variations will be listed.

Suddenly a bird is disturbed in front of you. How big was it? Always err slightly on the small size. If you think it was the size of a Blackbird (25 cm or 10 in), start with the 22 cm (8–9 in) long birds and progress through the pages until you see the one that looks similar. Check the **Primary Features**. If it tallies with what you have seen, you have identified the bird from a minimum of detail. The rest of the information should reinforce your identification and also make you aware of similar birds with different specific features.

Good birdwatching, and don't forget to tick off your sightings on the checklist provided with the index!

Specimen Spread

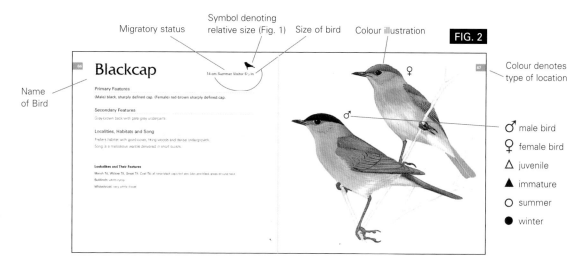

Migratory status

Symbol denoting relative size (Fig. 1)

Size of bird

Colour illustration

FIG. 2

Name of Bird

Colour denotes type of location

♂ male bird

♀ female bird

△ juvenile

▲ immature

○ summer

● winter

66

Blackcap

14 cm Summer Visitor 5½ in

Primary Features

(Male) black, sharply defined cap. (Female) red-brown sharply defined cap.

Secondary Features

Grey-brown back with pale grey underparts.

Localities, Habitats and Song

Prefers habitat with good cover, liking woods and dense undergrowth.

Song is a melodious warble delivered in short bursts.

Lookalikes and Their Features

Marsh Tit, Willow Tit, Great Tit, Coal Tit: all have black caps but also bibs and black areas around neck.

Bullfinch: white rump.

Whitethroat: very white throat.

♀

♂

67

Colour photograph offering an alternative angle, showing the bird in its typical habitat.

Glossary of Terms

Adult

A mature bird capable of breeding.

Bib

A distinctively coloured patch of feathers
in the throat and upper breast region,
e.g. Coal Tit.

Call-note

A few notes, or even a single note,
indicating alarm or acting as a simple
statement of presence.

Decurved

Curved downwards, e.g. the bill of the Curlew.

Display

A ritualised pattern of behaviour, usually
movement, by which birds communicate with
each other, particularly during courtship and in
defence of territory.

Female

Otherwise known as the hen (general), duck
(ducks), goose (geese) or pen (swans).

Feral

Established in a wild state but originating from
domesticated stock.

Immature

A fully grown bird but not yet old enough to
breed; immature plumage may be distinctively
different from adult.

Juvenile

A young bird in its own first plumage variation,
having left the nest but not yet completed its
first moult at the end of the summer.

Male

Otherwise known as the cock (general), drake
(ducks), gander (geese) or cob (swans).

Mask

A distinctively coloured patch of feathers on the
cheek and around the eyes, often joined, if only
thinly, across the forehead, e.g. Lesser Whitethroat.

Passage migrant

A migratory species, usually seen briefly in spring
and/or autumn, en route to its breeding
or wintering grounds, e.g. Knot.

Resident

Present throughout the year, e.g. Blackbird;
the resident population may be supplemented
at certain times of the year by individuals from
abroad, e.g. Starling.

Shield

A structure, lacking feathers, on the forehead of some waterbirds, e.g. Coot.

Song

A sustained and consistent collection of notes, a trill or a warble, used principally to proclaim ownership of territory, particularly during the breeding season.

Spatulate

Having a long, spread and flattened shape, e.g. the bill of the Shoveler.

Species

A group of individuals (population) whose members resemble each other more closely than they resemble members of other populations and which, almost invariably, are capable of breeding only amongst themselves.

Speculum

A panel on the trailing edge of the inner wing feathers of ducks, usually highly and distinctively coloured.

Sub-species

A group of individuals within a species which differ slightly, usually in plumage, from the typical form but which are capable of breeding with any individual of that species.

Summer visitor

A migratory species, arriving in spring and returning to its winter home at the end of the breeding season, e.g. Swallow.

Tube-nosed

Having nostrils in the form of slightly raised tubes running forwards from the extreme base of the bill, e.g. Fulmar.

Wing-bar

A relatively narrow band of colour along the length of the wing, e.g. Chaffinch.

Wing flash

A relatively narrow band of colour across the width of the wing, e.g. Wood Pigeon.

Wing patch

A relatively large area of colour on the wing, e.g. Greenfinch.

Winter visitor

A migratory species, arriving in late autumn and returning to its summer home to breed when conditions there improve in spring, e.g. Redwing.

The Parts of a Bird

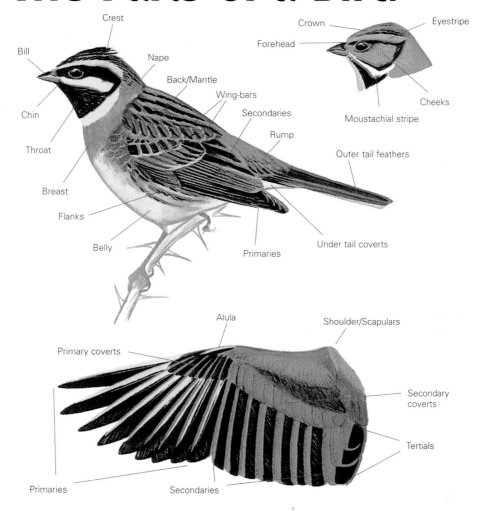

Crest

Crown

Eyestripe

Bill

Forehead

Nape

Back/Mantle

Wing-bars

Chin

Secondaries

Cheeks

Throat

Rump

Moustachial stripe

Breast

Outer tail feathers

Flanks

Belly

Primaries

Under tail coverts

Alula

Shoulder/Scapulars

Primary coverts

Secondary coverts

Tertials

Primaries

Secondaries

Goldcrest

9 cm Resident **3½ in**

Primary Features

Tiny bird with yellow crown edged with black.

Secondary Features

Plump, active bird with olive-green back and off-white underparts. Two white wing-bars.

Localities, Habitats and Song

Prefers coniferous woodlands, sometimes in evergreen hedges and bushes in gardens.

Actively searches for small insects, mainly in the higher branches. Not shy of man.

Lookalikes and Their Features

(**Firecrest:** almost identical; prominent white stripe between black edge of crown and eye.)

Warblers and **tits:** beware – similar size and flitting, foraging behaviour may confuse, especially high in the trees.

However, markings of Goldcrest are distinctive.

A Goldcrest returns to its nest. This tiny yet distinctive bird prefers coniferous woodland but sometimes nests in evergreen hedges, such as the pine here.

Wren

10 cm Resident **4 in**

Primary Features

Tiny brown bird with upright tail.

Secondary Features

Brown plumage closely barred, darker above and paler below.

Distinctive, straight, rapid flight on whirring wings, and surprisingly powerful song.

Localities, Habitats and Song

One of our commonest birds, found mostly in areas with dense, low cover.

Particularly favours ivy thickets in which to build its domed nest.

Lookalikes and Their Features

None.

A very common bird, the Wren is distinctive because of its upright tail and powerful song.

Willow Warbler

11 cm Summer Visitor **4¹/₂ in**

Primary Features

No wing-bars and (April–July) musical song consisting of descending sequence of notes ending in a flourish.

Secondary Features

Pale eye-stripe and olive-green back. Intensity of yellow underparts varies according to individual and season. Paler belly. Legs generally light brown but very variable. Call (not song) repeated di-syllabic 'hoo-eet'.

Localities, Habitats and Song

Commons, heaths and lightly wooded land are preferred habitat for this numerous summer visitor.

Lookalikes and Their Features

Chiffchaff: so similar that most observers call both 'Willow-Chiffs'; song: distinctive, repeated 'chiffchaff', and call: single-syllable 'hweet'; legs generally dark.

(**Wood Warbler:** yellow-green back; bright yellow breast; white belly; prefers woods.)

Chiffchaff

11 cm Summer Visitor **4¹/₂ in**

Primary Features

No wing-bars. Song is a repeated 'chiffchaff, chiffchaff'.

Secondary Features

Pale eye-stripe and olive-green back. Underparts yellow, varying in intensity according to individual and season. Belly paler. Legs usually dark. Call (as opposed to song) is a one-syllable 'hweet'.

Localities, Habitats and Song

Inhabits woods and thick undergrowth.

Lookalikes and Their Features

Willow Warbler: so similar that most observers are content to call both 'Willow-Chiffs'; generally legs paler brown and colours slightly brighter; song: distinctive, prolonged, musical warble; call: di-syllabic 'hoo-eet'.

(**Wood Warbler:** yellow-green back; bright yellow breast; white belly.)

The yellow underparts of the Chiffchaff vary in intensity depending on the time of year and the individual bird.

Coal Tit

11 cm Resident **4¹/₂ in**

Primary Features

White patch on nape and buff belly.

Secondary Features

Glossy black crown and white cheeks. Two white wing-bars and olive-grey back.

Localities, Habitats and Song

The smallest tit, inhabits woods and gardens. Very common, often flocking with other tit species.

Lookalikes and Their Features

Great Tit: much larger; yellow belly with prominent black stripe; green back.

Marsh and Willow Tits: lack white nape and white wing-bars.

Blue Tit: blue crown and yellow belly.

Blue Tit

11 cm Resident **4¹/₂ in**

Primary Features

Blue crown and yellow belly.

Secondary Features

Blue wings and tail. Fine stripe down belly. White cheeks and border to blue crown. Green back.

Localities, Habitats and Song

Extremely acrobatic in searching for insects on twigs and branches.

Very common in woods, gardens and hedgerows; often flocks with other tits.

Lookalikes and Their Features

Great Tit: larger; black crown; white cheeks; prominent black stripe down belly.

Coal Tit: black crown; white nape; lacks stripe on buff belly.

A Blue Tit in flight, revealing its yellow belly and beautiful blue wings. Blue Tits are extremely acrobatic.

Marsh Tit

11 cm Resident **4^1/$_2$ in**

Primary Features

Glossy black cap and no wing-bars or pale patch on wing.

Secondary Features

Brown back. Off-white cheeks and underparts. Small black bib.

Localities, Habitats and Song

Woodland bird, preferring deciduous trees. Typical tit, flitting along branches seeking insects.

Lookalikes and Their Features

Willow Tit: almost identical but has dull cap and pale patch on inner wing.

Coal Tit: white patch on nape; buff belly.

Blackcap (male): grey back; lacks black bib.

Willow Tit

11 cm Resident **4^1/$_2$ in**

Primary Features

Dull black cap and light patch on inner wing.

Secondary Features

Brown back, off-white cheeks and underparts. Small black bib.

Localities, Habitats and Song

Despite name, prefers wet woodlands and marshy areas with trees, though often occurs with Marsh Tit which generally favours drier habitats.

Lookalikes and Their Features

Marsh Tit: almost identical but has glossy cap and lacks light patch on inner wing.

Coal Tit: white patch on nape; buff belly.

Blackcap (male): grey back; lacks black bib.

House Martin

13 cm Summer Visitor **5 in**

Primary Features

Reminiscent of a Swallow but with white rump.

Secondary Features

Blue-black crown, back, wings and forked tail. White underparts. White feathered legs.

Localities, Habitats and Song

Common around buildings but also in open country. Like others of the Swallow family, usually seen on the wing in pursuit of insects. May settle on the ground, particularly to collect mud to build a nest under the eaves of a house.

Lookalikes and Their Features

Swallow: long, forked tail; red face.

Sand Martin: brown back and band on breast; lacks white rump.

Swift: scythe-like wings; almost completely brown-black.

Treecreeper

13 cm Resident **5 in**

Primary Features

Downward-curved bill.

Secondary Features

Small, active, mouse-like bird. Brown with white underparts, white eye-stripe and buff wing-bars.

Localities, Habitats and Song

Aptly named, usually seen climbing tree trunks in search of insects using stiff tail feathers as a support, like a Woodpecker. Motion is jerky and only rarely descends trees. Primarily a woodland bird though may visit garden trees.

Lookalikes and Their Features

None.

As its name suggests, the Treecreeper is excellent at climbing trees. Its tail feathers provide essential support.

Nuthatch

14 cm Resident **5¹/₂ in**

Primary Features

Able to climb on tree trunks in any direction.

Secondary Features

Distinctive plumage with blue-grey crown, back and tail, pale buff underparts, chestnut flanks and prominent black eye-stripe.

Localities, Habitats and Song

Small, stumpy-tailed bird with awkward, jerky flight, usually confined to short distances between trees. Found in deciduous woodland and gardens where it finds and hoards nuts, acorns and insects.

Lookalikes and Their Features

None.

Long-Tailed Tit

14 cm Resident **5¹/₂ in**

Primary Features

Mainly black and white with some pink plumage and very long, 7.5 cm (3 in), tail.

Secondary Features

Black crown with white stripe in centre. Face and breast white. Belly, flanks, rump and mid-back pink. Wings and tail black edged with white.

Localities, Habitats and Song

Inhabits woodlands and hedgerows. Restless, acrobatic bird, often flocking with other tits.

Lookalikes and Their Features

Pied Wagtail: lacks pink plumage; generally seen feeding on the ground in open country; runs in a series of stops and starts.

Robin

14 cm Resident **5¹/₂ in**

Primary Features

Bright orange-red plumage from forehead to breast.

Secondary Features

Green-brown above with pale grey margin around forehead and breast, shading to buff below.

Localities, Habitats and Song

Melodic warbling song usually given from prominent perch. Very common in gardens and woods. Despite 'friendly' nature suggested by their bold attitude to people, they are very aggressive in defending territories from each other.

Lookalikes and Their Features

Redstart: orange-brown tail, frequently flicked upwards.

The bold Robin is not afraid of humans and is therefore a common sight in gardens of Britain. A very popular bird, it has a melodic warbling song.

Blackcap

14 cm Summer Visitor **5¹/₂ in**

Primary Features

Male: black, sharply defined cap. Female: red-brown sharply defined cap.

Secondary Features

Grey-brown back with pale grey underparts.

Localities, Habitats and Song

Prefers habitat with good cover, liking woods and dense undergrowth.

Song is a melodious warble delivered in short bursts.

Lookalikes and Their Features

Marsh Tit, Willow Tit, Great Tit, Coal Tit: all have black caps but also bibs and black areas around neck.

Bullfinch: white rump.

Whitethroat: very white throat.

A female Blackcap. The only difference between the sexes is that the male has a sharply defined 'black cap' while the female's is red-brown in colour.

Redstart

14 cm Summer Visitor **5¹/₂ in**

Primary Features

Orange-brown tail which flicks frequently upwards. Male has white forehead.
Female has buff underparts.

Secondary Features

Male has black face and throat with orange-red underparts and a grey back.
Female is nondescript with grey-brown upper parts.

Localities, Habitats and Song

An active restless bird whose short, fluttering flights and general behaviour are reminiscent
of the Robin. Though widespread on heaths and in woodlands it is patchily distributed and
easily overlooked.

Lookalikes and Their Features

(**Black Redstart:** (male) no white forehead or orange-red underparts; (female) darker and greyer.)

Robin: no black face or white forehead.

Stonechat: (male) white neck-patch on black head; (female) darker, white wing-patches, dark tail.

(**Nightingale:** larger; skulking; liquid song.)

Garden Warbler

14 cm Summer Visitor **5$\frac{1}{2}$ in**

Primary Features

Brown bird, paler below and darker above, with unique lack of wing or tail markings and no eye-stripe.

Secondary Features

This very nondescript bird is characterised by its lack of features. Slightly plumper than similar warblers with a pleasing, gentle expression. Tail square-ended.

Localities, Habitats and Song

Found in both woodland and open heath, its sustained warbling song often betrays its presence.

Lookalikes and Their Features

Reed Warbler: more slender; rounded tail; prefers marshy habitat.

Willow Warbler and Chiffchaff: distinct eye-stripe.

Whitethroat: very white throat; rufous wings.

The Garden Warbler is a plain bird with very few markings. It can be found in woods and on heathland.

Spotted Flycatcher

14 cm Summer Visitor **5¹/₂ in**

Primary Features

Flycatching behaviour and streaked (not spotted) breast.

Secondary Features

Unobtrusively marked. Light grey-brown back and tail, and pale breast. Brown streaks on crown, forehead and breast.

Localities, Habitats and Song

Preys on insects from a post or other prominent place. Darts from perch, twisting and turning acrobatically to catch an insect before returning to same perch. Found from April–September in woodland and large gardens.

Lookalikes and Their Features

Warblers: similarly slender with nondescript plumage only distinguishable on close view.

Lacks the unmistakable flycatching behaviour.

Great Tit

14 cm Resident **5¹/₂ in**

Primary Features

Black stripe down belly (broader in male).

Secondary Features

Yellow belly. White cheeks. Black bib typical of tits. Sexes similar.

Localities, Habitats and Song

Largest of the tit family. Very common. Frequents woods, gardens and hedgerows.

Often flocks with other tits outside breeding season.

Lookalikes and Their Features

Blue Tit: much smaller; blue crown, wings and tail; fine, blue belly stripe.

Coal Tit: smaller; prominent white nape; white cheeks; black crown; buff belly without stripe.

The Great Tit can often be seen in flocks with other tits and is very common in woods, gardens and hedgerows.

Greenfinch

15 cm Resident **5³/₄ in**

Primary Features

Olive-green plumage with bright yellow patches on wing.

Secondary Features

Adults of both sexes have yellow-green rump and yellow patches on tail. Females and juveniles duller than male, and juveniles show strong streaks above and below.

Localities, Habitats and Song

Frequents gardens and open farmland.

Lookalikes and Their Features

(**Siskin:** smaller; male has black crown, female strongly streaked below.)

Goldfinch: distinctive yellow wing-bars; confusion unlikely except at long range.

A female Greenfinch is duller in colour than the male but still has bright yellow patches on her tail.

House Sparrow

15 cm Resident 5³/₄ **in**

Primary Features

Male has grey crown with a black bib. Female is nondescript with pale eye-stripe.
Usually in close association with male.

Secondary Features

Male has brown back streaked with black; brown nape and pale grey cheeks and white wing-bar.
Grey rump and pale grey underparts. Female has duller brown back than male, but is also streaked.

Localities, Habitats and Song

Well known for its tameness in towns, but also common on farmland, often in flocks and in association with finches. Both sparrows and finches have deep bills typical of birds which eat grain.

Lookalikes and Their Features

Tree Sparrow: chocolate-brown crown with black cheek spots; white collar.

Dunnock: (often called Hedge Sparrow) very different build; slender bill; no pale cheeks.

A male House Sparrow can be identified by its black bib. The female of the species is plainer in colour.

Dunnock

15 cm Resident **6 in**

Primary Features

Grey head markings and underparts with a slender bill.

Secondary Features

Brown back streaked black as the two true sparrows. The Dunnock is often misnamed Hedge Sparrow.

Localities, Habitats and Song

Shy, even skulking manner. Plump Robin-like build and delicate flight are totally distinctive.

A solitary bird, it is normally found on the ground under bushes, hedgerows, etc.

Lookalikes and Their Features

House Sparrow: grey crown; black bib.

Tree Sparrow: chocolate-brown crown; black spot on cheek.

The Dunnock has a plump build similar to that of a Robin. A shy bird, it is normally found under bushes and hedgerows.

Swift

17 cm Summer Visitor **6¹/₂ in**

Primary Features

Narrow scythe-like wings.

Secondary Features

Uniformly brown-black swallow-like bird with small white throat patch. Tail is forked but without streamers.

Localities, Habitats and Song

Totally aerial except during the breeding season, at the nest, and if exhausted, in which case weak legs and long wings prevent take-off from the ground and bird usually dies. Flight is rapid and jerky in pursuit of prey.

Lookalikes and Their Features

Swallow: pale underparts; red face; (in adult) tail streamers.

House Martin: pale underparts and white rump.

Sand Martin: pale underparts; brown bar on breast.

Starling

22 cm Resident **8¹/₂ in**

Primary Features

Spangled body plumage, which in summer is iridescent, and in winter is white-speckled.

Secondary Features

Plump bodied with short, pointed wings. Juveniles initially are uniform mouse-brown, progressing to adult plumage.

Localities, Habitats and Song

May fly large distances daily in immense flocks. Famed for remarkable ability to mimic other birds' songs in addition to its own guttural warbles and whistles.

Lookalikes and Their Features

None.

Great Spotted Woodpecker

23 cm Resident **9–9¹/₂ in**

Primary Features

Pied plumage with prominent white shoulder patches.

Secondary Features

Black crown, white cheeks, crimson on nape (male only) and under tail. Black back, white shoulders, and barred white-on-black wings give striking pied effect in flight. Underparts buff-white.

Localities, Habitats and Song

Widespread in mixed woodland, parks and secluded gardens. Loud, fast 'drumming' with bill on trees. Flight highly undulating.

Lookalikes and Their Features

(Lesser Spotted Woodpecker: much smaller (Sparrow-sized); white bars instead of patches on shoulder; crimson head (male only).)

The Great Spotted Woodpecker stands out because of its crimson plumage and the unmistakable drumming noise it makes.

Song Thrush

23 cm Resident **9 in**

Primary Features

Typical thrush with speckled breast and orange underwing.

Secondary Features

Warm brown back and head.

Localities, Habitats and Song

Common garden bird with direct flight. Often seen cracking snail shells open on stones.

Builds a mud-lined nest in garden hedgerows for its sky-blue and black spotted eggs.

Lookalikes and Their Features

Mistle Thrush: larger; head greyer; white underwing and outer tail feathers.

Redwing: smaller; white eye-stripe; red flanks and underwing.

Fieldfare: grey head; brown back; grey rump; white underwing.

The Song Thrush can often be seen cracking snail shells and is a frequent garden dweller.

Blackbird

25 cm Resident **10 in**

Primary Features

The male is a uniformly black garden bird; while the female is uniformly brown.

Secondary Features

Male has yellow bill and eye-rings. Female has light speckling on the breast and yellow eye-rings.

Localities, Habitats and Song

Probably Britain's commonest garden bird, found in gardens everywhere.

Formerly common in ancestral, woodland habitat.

Lookalikes and Their Features

(**Ring Ouzel:** white gorget or band across upper breast.)

A male Blackbird feeds his young. The female of the species is brown rather than black.

Mistle Thrush

27 cm Resident **10¹/₂–11 in**

Primary Features

Thrush with grey-brown head and white outer tail feathers.

Secondary Features

Typical speckled breast, with greyish brown back and head. White underwing.

Localities, Habitats and Song

Usually seen on playing fields and parks but also common in wooded areas. Less common in gardens. Country name 'Stormcock' from its habit of singing from a high perch in blustery or stormy conditions.

Lookalikes and Their Features

Song Thrush: smaller, orange underwing; browner back.

Redwing: smaller; white eye-stripe; red flanks and underwing.

Fieldfare: grey head; brown back; grey rump.

The Mistle Thrush is also known as a 'Stormcock' and can be seen in playing fields and parks as well as wooded areas.

Collared Dove

32 cm Resident **12¹/₂ in**

Primary Features

Zig-zag collar markings.

Secondary Features

A grey-brown backed dove with blue-grey wings. Broad white band on tail shows especially when alighting. Black collar is edged with white.

Localities, Habitats and Song

Most usually seen in parks and wooded gardens; also in larger flocks on smallholdings and farmland.

Lookalikes and Their Features

(**Turtle Dove:** orange-brown back feathers with black centres; pied patch on neck.)

Feral Pigeon: no black and white collar.

Wood Pigeon: green and white patches on neck; white flashes on wing.

So-called because of its zig-zag markings around the neck, the Collared Dove has beautiful blue-grey wings.

Green Woodpecker

30–33 cm Resident **12–13 in**

Primary Features

Green with crimson crown.

Secondary Features

A very distinctive bird. Yellow rump contrasts with green in unmistakable, undulating flight. Pale underparts and black patch on face.

Localities, Habitats and Song

Makes loud tapping rather than loud drumming of Spotted Woodpeckers. Its nickname 'Yaffle' comes from its loud, laughing call. Feeds mainly on the ground in deciduous woods, parks and gardens.

Lookalikes and Their Features

None.

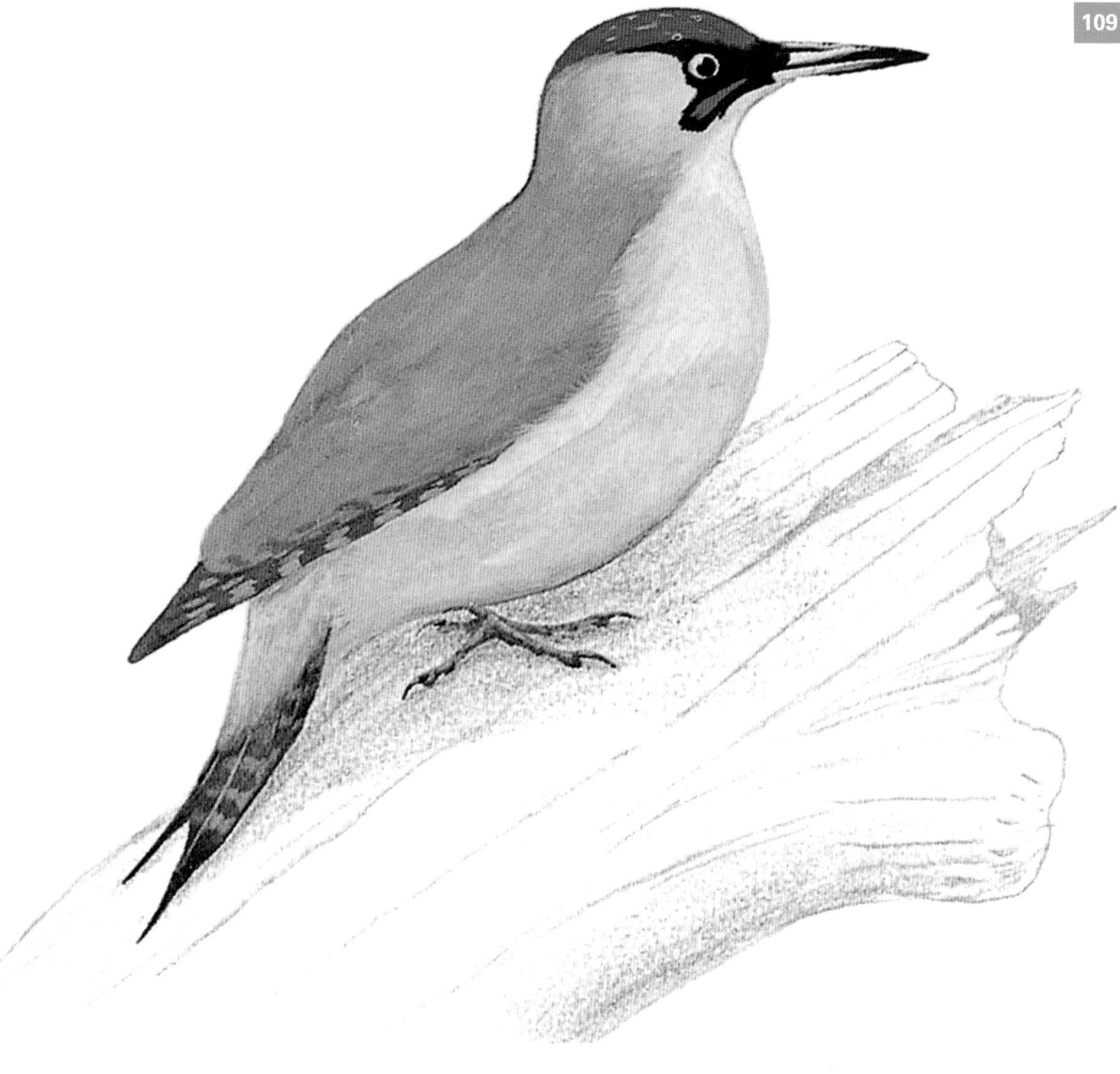

The Green Woodpecker was given the nickname 'Yaffle' because of its loud, laughing call.

Feral Pigeon

33 cm Resident **13 in**

Primary Features

Town pigeons with a fast direct flight and 'oor-coo-coo' call.

Secondary Features

Plumage very variable. Those most like wild ancestors are grey with white rump and two large black wing-bars. Other common varieties are black, brown and white or mottled grey, often without the white rump. Wings long and pointed.

Localities, Habitats and Song

May form large flocks in towns and on farmland where damage to crops may result. Their large, messy nests are a common sight on buildings and statues. Probably derived from domesticated Rock Doves.

Lookalikes and Their Features

Stock Dove: pinkish throat and breast; no black borders on underwing.

Wood Pigeon: white flashes on wing; white neck-patch; pink breast.

Collared Dove: white band on tail; zig-zag mark on neck.

(**Turtle Dove:** white tail-band; pied neck markings.)

Jackdaw

33 cm Resident **13 in**

Primary Features

Grey nape.

Secondary Features

This black bird is frequently confused with the larger crows and rooks, despite clear grey nape and unmistakable call-note, a ringing 'chack'.

Localities, Habitats and Song

Favours woods and buildings, but also frequents sea and inland cliffs where nesting holes can be found. According to legend jackdaws love to steal bright objects.

Lookalikes and Their Features

Carrion Crow: larger; all black.

Rook: larger with pale grey face.

Black-Headed Gull

35–38 cm Resident **14–15 in**

Primary Features

In summer has chocolate brown head and in winter has dark ear spots and red legs.

Secondary Features

Red bill and legs (may fade to orange in winter); grey back and upper wings with broad white leading edge and black tips. Immatures and juveniles show varying amounts of brown on upper parts and black tip to the tail.

Localities, Habitats and Song

Common on coasts. Most widespread of gulls inland.

Lookalikes and Their Features

(Winter) **Common Gull:** yellow bill and legs; no ear spot.

Herring Gull: flesh-coloured legs; no ear spot.

Kittiwake: no white on wing tip; black legs.

(Summer) **Arctic Tern** and **Common Tern:** black-capped; forked tail.

The Black-Headed Gull develops dark ear spots during the winter months and its red bill also fades to orange.

Jay

36 cm Resident **14 in**

Primary Features

Bright blue wing-patches with black bands.

Secondary Features

White rump most conspicuous as bird flies away; wings black and white above with blue patch on coverts; body mainly pink; head has black and white crest and dark moustache-like streak.

Localities, Habitats and Song

Very shy and wary, it is most likely to be seen in slow and clumsy flight. Fond of woodland, it is agile in trees and may hop on ground. The most colourful of the crow family.

Lookalikes and Their Features

None.

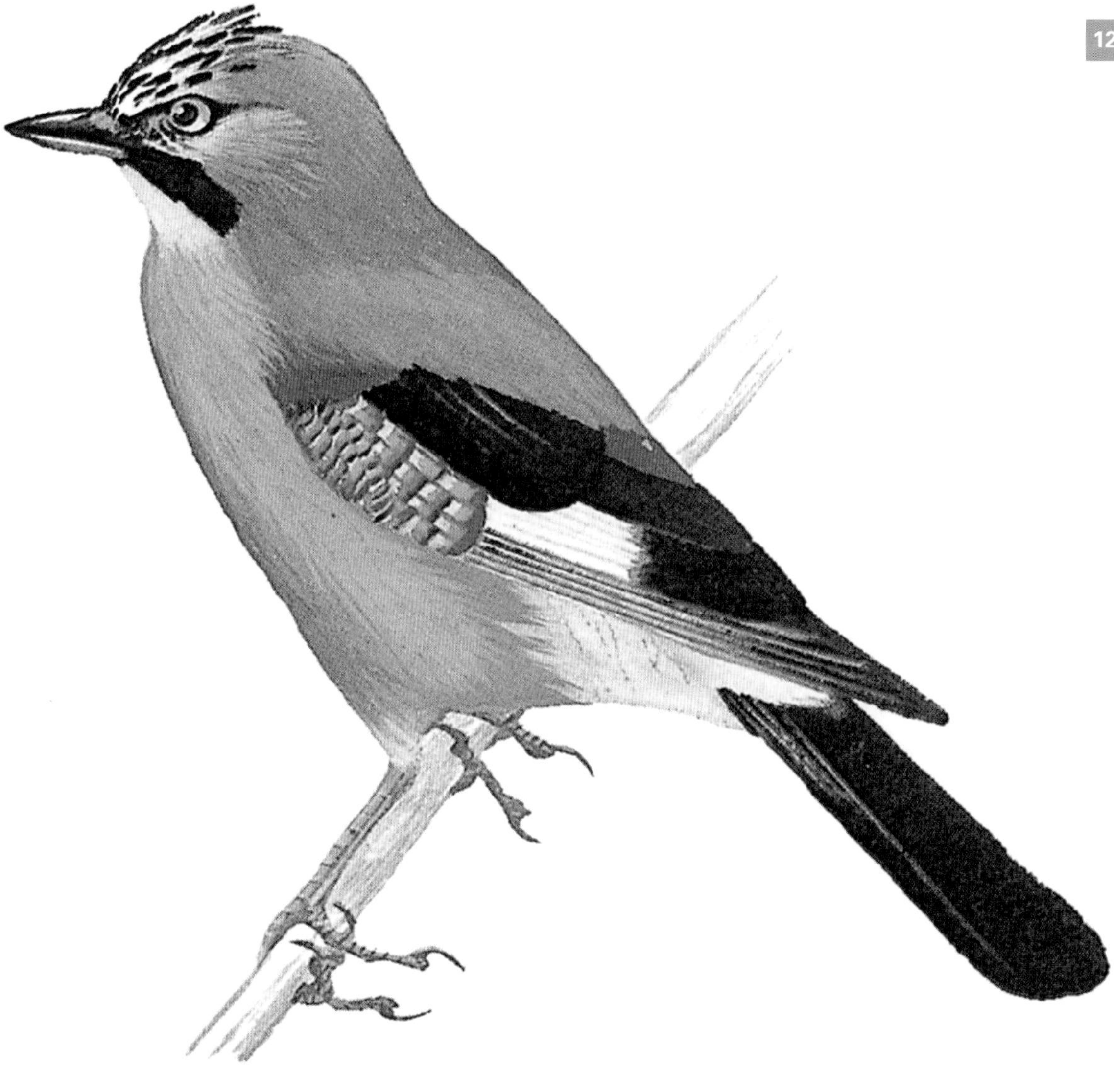

Tawny Owl

38 cm Resident **15 in**

Primary Features

Distinctive hooting call and flight call. Very large head in proportion to body.

Secondary Features

Mottled brown back and upper wings; underparts and underwings buff streaked with brown. Mid-upper wing (scapulars) has white spots. Large black eyes, no ear tufts and short broad rounded wings.

Localities, Habitats and Song

Entirely nocturnal. Only flies by day when disturbed. Only in woodlands. Song is the 'hoo-hoo-hoo-hooooo' of the storybook owl. Flight-call a distinctive 'ker-wick'.

Lookalikes and Their Features

(Short-Eared Owl: flies by day; pale underwing with black carpal (midwing) patches.)

Barn Owl: pale or white face and underwing.

A pair of Tawny Owl chicks huddle together. Note their short wings and large black eyes.

Common Gull

41 cm Resident **16 in**

Primary Features

Pale grey back and yellow legs.

Secondary Features

Slim gull with white head, belly, underwings and tail. Black wing ends with white tips and lightweight bill with no red spot. Streaked neck in winter. Immature and juveniles show varying degrees of brown on back.

Localities, Habitats and Song

Coastal as other gulls and also inland, particularly on park and arable land. Not in fact the most common gull.

Lookalikes and Their Features

Herring Gull: larger; heavier bill with red spot; flesh-coloured legs.

Black-Headed Gull: (winter) black ear spot; red bill and legs; broad white leading edge to wing.

Kittiwake: no white on wing tips; black legs.

Fulmar: straight wings without black tips; tube-like nostrils.

Wood Pigeon

41 cm Resident **16 in**

Primary Features

White wing-flashes and neck-patch.

Secondary Features

Our largest pigeon. Grey back and inner wing; blue-grey head, rump and belly; outer wing and tail tip black; green patch next to white neck patch; pinkish breast. From below white band across middle of black tail.

Localities, Habitats and Song

Generally frequents woods, though also gardens and farmland (where large flocks may gather). Takes flight noisily when disturbed. Flight is fast and direct, but when displaying climbs steeply to glide down on V-shaped wings.

Lookalikes and Their Features

Stock Dove, Feral Pigeon: lack white wing-flashes and neck patch.

Collared Dove: lacks white wing-patches, has zig-zag neck marking.

(**Turtle Dove:** lacks white wing-flashes, has pied neck markings.)

The Wood Pigeon is Britain's largest pigeon and is easily distinguishable from the Feral Pigeon because of its white neck-patch.

Magpie

46 cm Resident **18 in**

Primary Features

Pied plumage with exceptionally long, wedge-ended tail.

Secondary Features

Black plumage is actually dark blue and dark green in parts. Otherwise bird is black except for white on belly, wing-tips and shoulder blades.

Localities, Habitats and Song

An unmistakable member of the crow family, found in woods and open spaces, gardens and thickets. It will eat almost anything, but is notorious as a robber of the eggs of smaller birds.

Lookalikes and Their Features

None.

The Magpie will eat almost anything and has a reputation for stealing eggs from other birds.

Carrion Crow

47 cm Resident **18¹/₂ in**

Primary Features

Entirely black with 'carr' call-note.

Secondary Features

Feathered around base of bill unlike Rook. In flight tail end is square not slightly wedge-shaped as Rook.

Localities, Habitats and Song

A scavenger, feeding on carrion, small mammals and birds, frogs, insects, vegetable matter, grain, etc. Hence occurs almost everywhere – one of the most familiar birds.

Lookalikes and Their Features

Rook: pale grey, unfeathered area at base of bill (in adult only).

Jackdaw: smaller; grey nape.

(Raven: much larger 63.5 cm (25 "); 'Pruk' call.)

Hooded Crow: sub-species replaces **Carrion Crow** in northern Britain; identical but for grey back and belly.

The Carrion Crow is a scavenger with a distinctive call-note that sounds like 'corr'.

Goldfinch

12 cm Resident **4³/₄ in**

Primary Features

Black wings with a broad bright yellow band.

Secondary Features

Adults have red, white and black markings on head, whilst head of juvenile is streaked brown. Rest of plumage mainly brown with pale underparts and rump; again juvenile is streaked. All ages have white spots on wing and tail tips.

Localities, Habitats and Song

Gathered into flocks, Goldfinches feed mainly on thistle seeds in winter fields and gardens. Song is a liquid twitter and the flight is undulating.

Lookalikes and Their Features

Greenfinch: yellow patch on wing; yellow outer tail feathers; only likely to be confused at a distance.

(**Siskin:** yellow on tail.)

♀

♂

The brightly coloured Goldfinch only develops its red, white and black markings when mature.

Sand Martin

12 cm Summer Visitor **4³/₄ in**

Primary Features

Swallow-type bird with brown bar across breast.

Secondary Features

Uniformly plain brown except for white underparts.

Localities, Habitats and Song

Smallest of the British Swallow-type birds, its method of feeding on the wing is typical, though its flight is less fluent. It nests in large colonies in burrows in sand cliffs or similar places.

Lookalikes and Their Features

House Martin: white rump.

Swallow: long, forked tail; red face.

Swift: scythe-shaped wings; no white underparts.

Sedge Warbler

13 cm Summer Visitor **5 in**

Primary Features

Very prominent eye-stripe and black-streaked crown.

Secondary Features

Small, plump warbler with streaked brown upper parts and creamy-coloured underparts.
Plain rump and tail.

Localities, Habitats and Song

Inhabits reed-beds and other thicket and hedge areas near water. Song is a remarkably loud, unmelodic churring. When not singing it skulks nimbly through thick vegetation. During courtship gives parachute display.

Lookalikes and Their Features

(**Grasshopper Warbler:** less prominent eye-stripe; strange mechanical 'reeling' song.)

Other **Warblers:** lack black streaks on crown; less prominent eye-stripes.

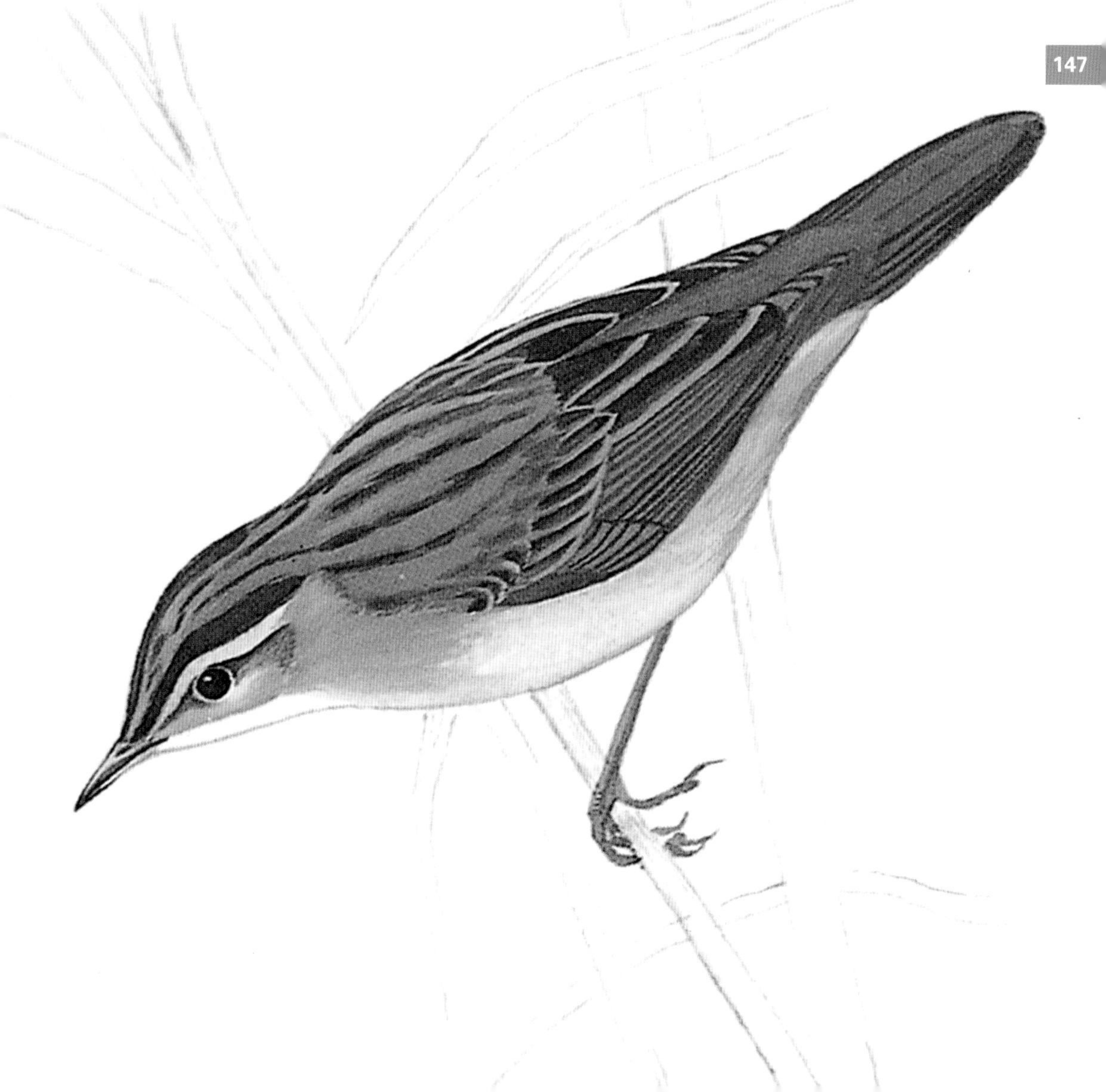

Reed Warbler

13 cm Summer Visitor **5 in**

Primary Features

Unmarked (i.e. no eye-stripe, back or crown streaks). Inhabits marshy areas.
Note lookalikes below.

Secondary Features

Warm rufous brown above with buff underparts and whitish throat. Rounded tail. Dark legs.

Localities, Habitats and Song

Usually found in reed-beds or other vegetation near water. Climbs restlessly in reeds where it builds remarkable suspended nest. Song is a repetitious churring and often gives first warning of bird's presence.

Lookalikes and Their Features

Female **Whitethroat:** prefers brambles, nettles and hedgerows.

Garden Warbler: plumper; woodland or heath habitat; square tail.

Other **Warblers:** Streaks, wing-bars or eye-stripes.

The ingenious Reed Warbler builds its nest so that it is suspended amongst the reeds of its favoured habitat.

Stonechat

13 cm Resident **5 in**

Primary Features

Male has head entirely black with white patch on side of neck and on wing. Female is brown with pale patch on wing. Consorts closely with male.

Secondary Features

Male has brown, streaked back and white rump. Chestnut underparts. Colours are duller outside breeding season. Female is duller version of male but lacks head, neck and rump markings.

Localities, Habitats and Song

Inhabits heaths, commons, waste-ground and open farmland, especially if gorse growing. Typically perches on tops of gorse bushes and fence posts. Its name comes from the call which sounds like two stones clicking together.

Lookalikes and Their Features

Whinchat: similar to female only; mainly brown; white eye-stripe and cheek outline.

Redstart: chestnut tail; male has white forehead.

Reed Bunting: white outer tail feathers; male has white moustache.

(**Pied Flycatcher:** white outer tail feathers; male black and white only.)

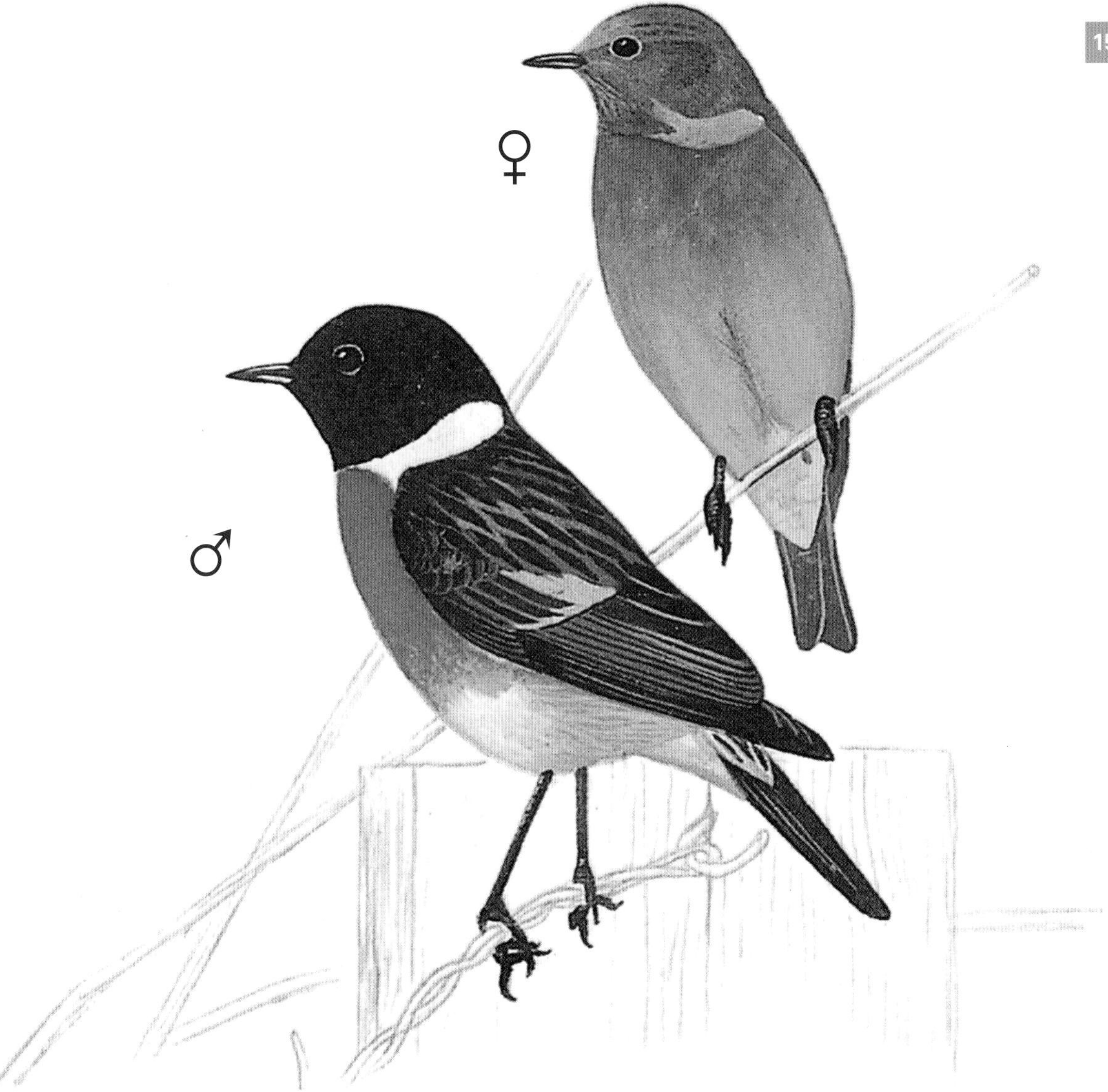

Whinchat

13 cm Summer Visitor **5 in**

Primary Features

White eye-stripe and border around cheek. Female duller than male.

Secondary Features

Back is brown and streaked. Underparts are buff. Sides of tail are white at the base. Only the male has the prominent white wing markings.

Localities, Habitats and Song

Prefers open country, grassland, heaths and gorse. Perches on prominent points with an upright posture, similar to its relative, the Stonechat. Flights between perches are short and rapid.

Lookalikes and Their Features

Stonechat: male has black head; both sexes lack white on tail feathers.

Sedge Warbler and other Warblers: eye-stripes are not white; lack white tail feathers.

♀

♂

Linnet

13 cm Resident **5¹/₄ in**

Primary Features

Male has crimson crown and breast. Female has white patches on wing, and consorts closely with male.

Secondary Features

Male has grey-brown head, brown back and buff underparts. Female is duller and streaked below. Both sexes and juveniles have white on the tail. Tail is markedly cleft.

Localities, Habitats and Song

Numerous on farmland and commons. The undulating flight and incessant twittering on the wing are good recognition features. Gregarious, they often associate with Greenfinches and Goldfinches.

Lookalikes and Their Features

(**Redpoll:** black spot under chin.)

(**Twite:** almost no white on wings and tail; male has pink rump.)

Chaffinch: two white wing-bars.

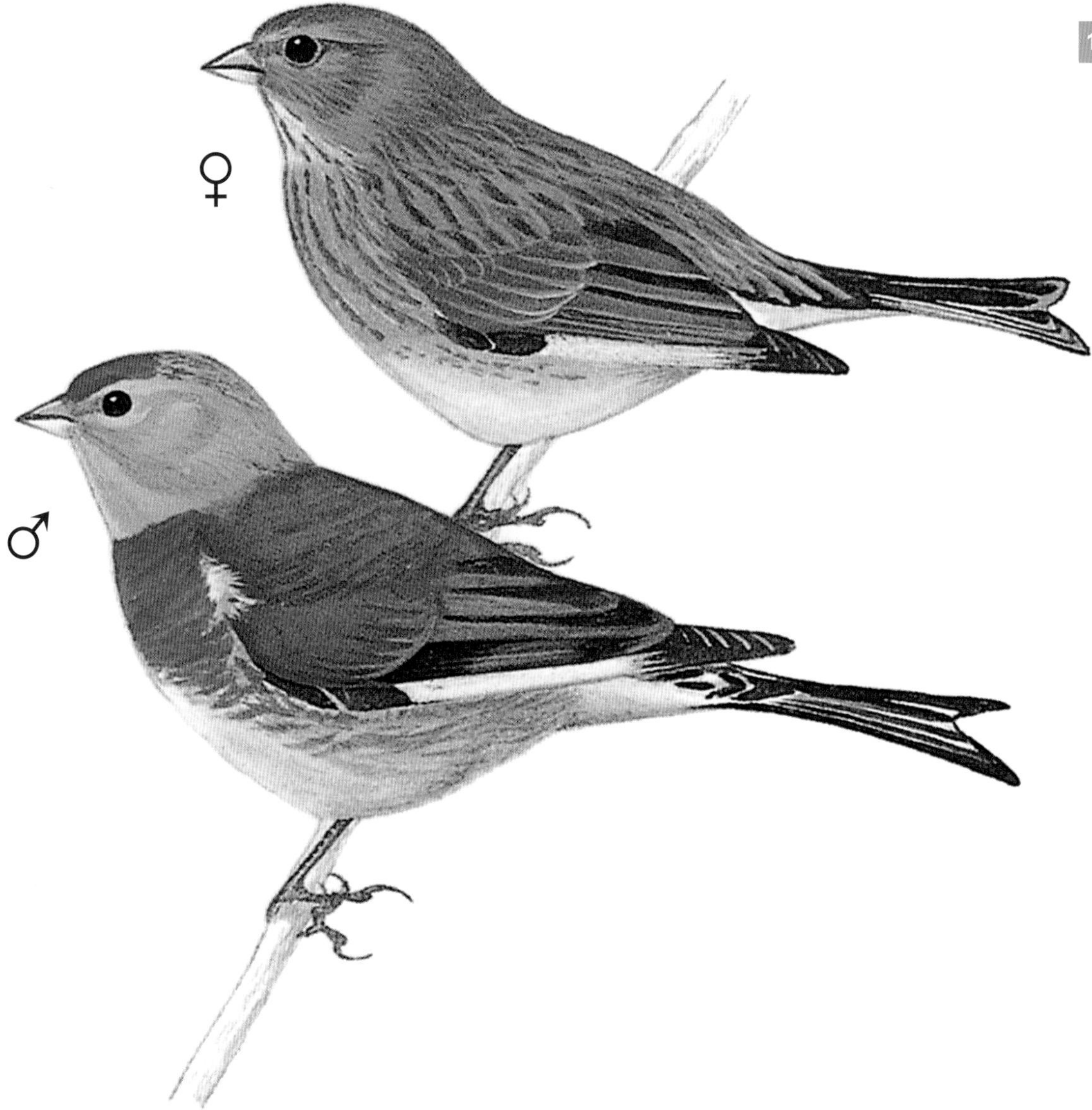

Linnets are particularly gregarious birds. This is a male – you can tell by its striking crimson plumage.

Tree Sparrow

14 cm Resident **5¹/₂ in**

Primary Features

Chocolate-brown crown and black spot on cheek.

Secondary Features

Brown-streaked back, pale grey cheeks and a small black bib. Pale grey underparts.

Localities, Habitats and Song

Unlike the House Sparrow, the Tree Sparrow mainly inhabits the countryside and is more wary of people.

Lookalikes and Their Features

House Sparrow: grey-brown; lacks cheek marking.

Dunnock: different shape; slender bill; lacks pale cheeks.

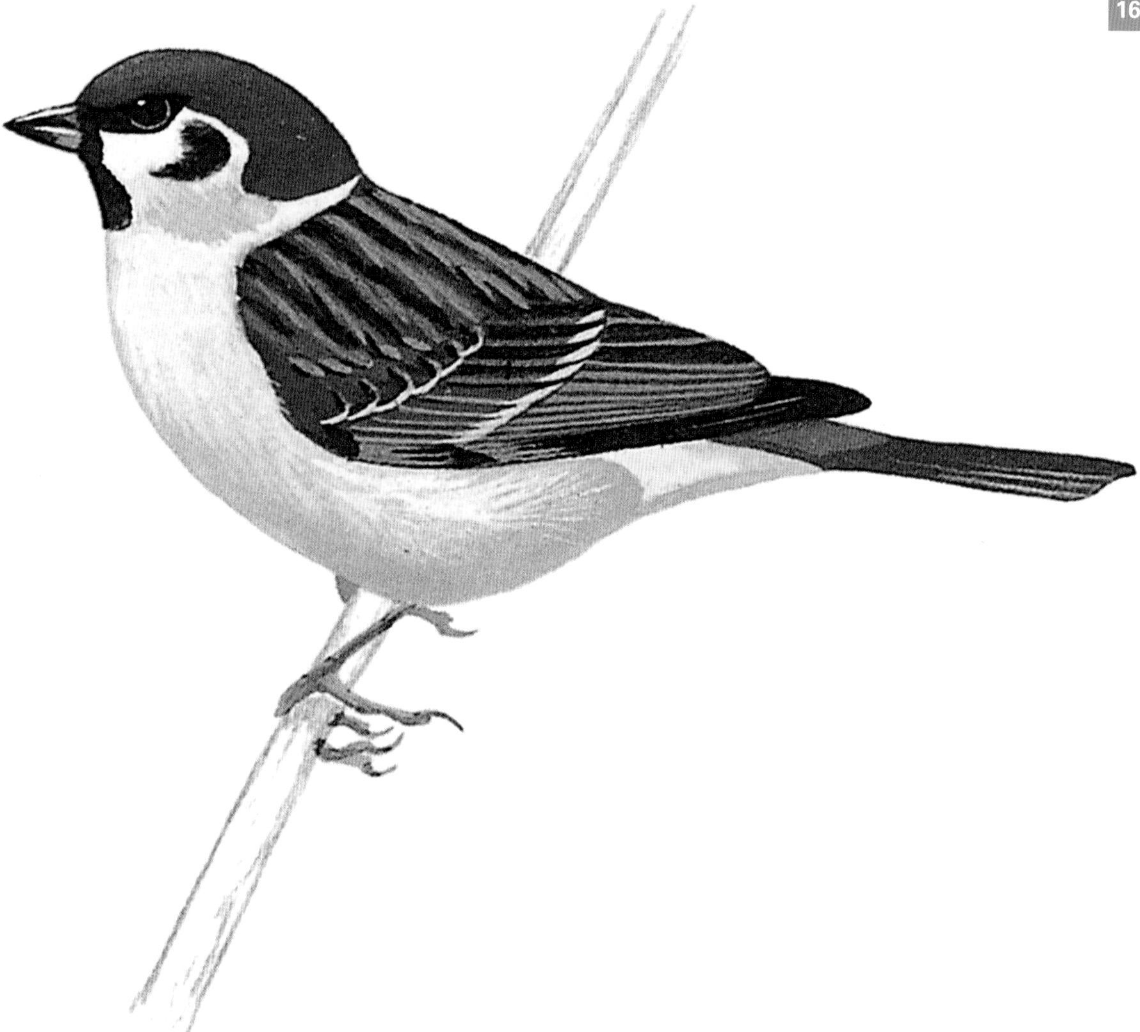

Whitethroat

14 cm Summer Visitor **5¹/₂ in**

Primary Features

White throat and outer tail feathers.

Secondary Features

Male has grey cap. His pale underparts are often noticeably pinkish. Female has brown cap and pale underparts. Both sexes have brown back and long tail. White outer tail feathers are distinctive but rarely seen.

Localities, Habitats and Song

Prefers tangled undergrowth such as nettles, brambles and hedgerows. Brief, jerky flight often ends in a vertical drop into cover.

Lookalikes and Their Features

(**Lesser Whitethroat**: lacks rufous wings; dark 'mask' around eyes.)

Blackcap (female): lacks white throat.

Reed Warbler: similar to female Whitethroat but prefers wet habitats.

Garden Warbler: grey-brown wings; grey throat.

Other **Warblers** and **Flycatchers:** eye-stripes and/or wing-bars.

The Whitethroat closely resembles members of the Warbler species but can be recognized by its white throat.

Bullfinch

15 cm Resident **5³/₄ in**

Primary Features

Black cap and white rump.

Secondary Features

Male has grey back and bright pink breast. Female has grey nape, brown back and breast.

Both sexes have black tail, black wings with faint white wing-bar and a heavy bill.

Juvenile as female but lacks black cap.

Localities, Habitats and Song

The bill is used for cracking seeds. Other foods include buds of fruit trees, making Bullfinches serious pests to fruit growers. Usually found in small woods and quiet gardens.

Lookalikes and Their Features

(**Brambling:** only similar in flight when white rump shows; lacks black cap; bright orange breast.)

Blackcap: lacks white rump.

Marsh and **Willow Tits:** lack white rump.

Redstart (male)**:** lacks white rump.

A Bullfinch family. The male is on the right – he has a brighter pink breast than the female.

Wheatear

15 cm Summer Visitor **5³/₄ in**

Primary Features

Black, inverted 'T' on a white rump and tail.

Secondary Features

Male has black mask, white eyebrow and grey crown and back. Female has pale eye-stripe and brown upper parts. Both sexes are buff below and have brown-black wings.

Localities, Habitats and Song

Distinctive, trim bird with attractive markings and upright stance. Inhabits barren open places such as cliff-tops, moorland and bleak pasture. Bobs tail like Wagtail.

Lookalikes and Their Features

Redstart: lacks pied rump and tail markings.

Whinchat: lacks pied rump and tail markings.

♀

♂

Chaffinch

15 cm Resident **5³/₄ in**

Primary Features

Double white wing-bars and white outer tail feathers that are very conspicuous in flight.

Secondary Features

Male has slate-blue crown, chestnut-brown back and pinkish face and breast. Female has greenish brown back, face and breast. Both sexes have green rump and blackish tail and wings.

Localities, Habitats and Song

Britain's commonest bird, numerous on farmland, hedgerows, woodland and gardens.
Often forms large flocks in winter. Flight is markedly undulating.

Lookalikes and Their Features

(**Brambling:** white rump, orange breast.)

Bullfinch: white rump; black cap.

Linnet: lacks wing-bars.

(**Twite:** lacks wing-bars.)

House Sparrow (female): single wing-bar; lacks white on tail.

A female Chaffinch. Like the male of the species she has double white wing-bars and a black tail.

Reed Bunting

15 cm Resident **6 in**

Primary Features

Heavy white moustache and white outer tail feathers.

Secondary Features

Male has black head and throat and white collar. Female has brown head, pale throat and pale eye-stripe. Both sexes have brown, streaked backs and heavily streaked, pale underparts. Juveniles similar but yellower colouring.

Localities, Habitats and Song

Prefers watery areas such as reed-beds, marshes and wet meadows, but also occurs on heaths and cultivated fields. Usually perches on high vegetation.

Lookalikes and Their Features

(Female **Cirl Bunting:** yellower; lacks white moustache.)

(**Corn Bunting:** lacks white outer tail feathers.)

Female **Yellowhammer:** yellower; chestnut rump.

Meadow Pipit: slimmer build; lacks moustache; beware similar call.

Meadow Pipit

15 cm Resident **6 in**

Primary Features

Similar to small Thrush with white outer tail feathers and weak 'tsip' call.

Secondary Features

Brown above, streaked with darker markings and pale, streaked breast. Pinkish legs with long hind claws.

Localities, Habitats and Song

Abundant in open country, tolerating the harshest of conditions. Flight is hesitant. Wags tail when walking. Forms flocks in winter.

Lookalikes and Their Features

(Tree Pipit: yellower breast; more powerful 'teeze' call-note.)

Rock Pipit: larger; darker plumage; dark legs.

Skylark: bulkier; crest.

Yellowhammer

17 cm Resident **6¹/₂ in**

Primary Features

Yellow head and chestnut rump.

Secondary Features

Brown streaked back and brown tail with white outer feathers. Underparts yellowish and streaked. Females are generally duller than males.

Localities, Habitats and Song

Abundant in farmland, hedgerows and on commons. Large flocks may form in autumn on stubble fields. Distinctive call often rendered as 'little bit of bread and no cheese'.

Lookalikes and Their Features

(**Cirl Bunting:** olive brown rump.)

Reed Bunting (female): lacks yellow colouring and chestnut rump.

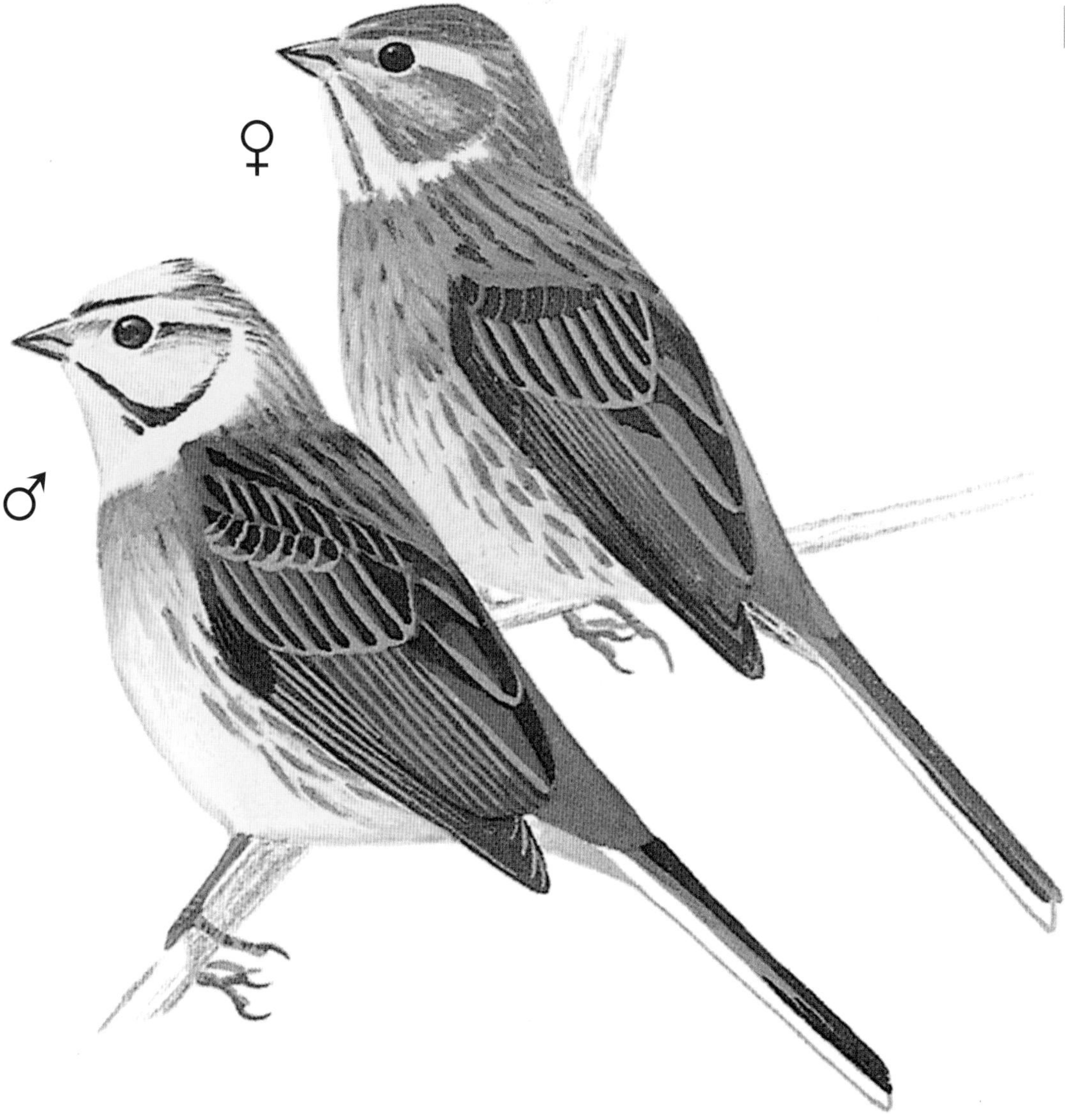

Blue-Headed and Yellow Wagtail

17 cm Summer Visitor **6¹/₂ in**

Primary Features

Blue-grey head and yellow throat (1), bright yellow face (2). Long tail which is repeatedly wagged.

Secondary Features

Yellow breast, prominent eyebrow stripe, olive-green back and rump. Black tail with white outer feathers. The Blue-Headed Wagtail (1) is a subspecies of the Yellow Wagtail (2), which is restricted to Britain.

Localities, Habitats and Song

Prefer wet habitats such as water meadows, sewage farms, etc., in which to find insect food. Also on comparatively dry heathland. Typical Wagtail behaviour of bobbing and darting, and undulating flight.

Lookalikes and Their Features

Grey Wagtail: grey face and back.

Kingfisher

17 cm Resident **6$^1/_2$ in**

Primary Features

Brilliant blue upper parts.

Secondary Features

The underparts and cheeks are chestnut. The throat and sides of the neck are white. The dagger-shaped beak contrasts with the short, stumpy body.

Localities, Habitats and Song

May be seen around any fresh water location, and occasionally saltwater in winter. Habitually feeds on fish obtained by diving from a favourite perch. Also takes insects. Nests in burrows, usually in stream banks.

Lookalikes and Their Features

None.

The dagger-shaped beak of the Kingfisher is clearly shown here. The size of the beak contrasts greatly with the birds' short body.

Skylark

18 cm Resident **7 in**

Primary Features

Similar to small Thrush but has crest and white outer tail feathers.

Secondary Features

Upper parts brown streaked with black. Pale underparts with black streaks on breast. Fairly long brown tail with white outer feathers.

Localities, Habitats and Song

Abundant in open country, the Skylark is most noted for its sustained song. It flies up to great heights to hang motionless while giving liquid, trilling outpourings. Bird may be so high as to be almost impossible to spot.

Lookalikes and Their Features

All **Pipits:** slimmer build; no crest.

Grey Wagtail

18 cm Resident **7 in**

Primary Features

Grey face and extraordinarily long tail which is repeatedly wagged.

Secondary Features

Grey back, greenish yellow rump, black tail with white outer feathers and yellow feathers under tail. Other underparts yellow in spring and summer, buff or white in autumn and winter. Male has white wing-bar and black bib. Female has white bib.

Localities, Habitats and Song

Almost invariably found by streams. Flicking of tail characteristic of all Wagtails, as are eccentric, dashing pursuit of insects and undulating flight.

Lookalikes and Their Features

Yellow Wagtail: olive-green back.

The Grey Wagtail is frequently found by streams flicking its incredibly long tail.

White and Pied Wagtail

18 cm Resident **7 in**

Primary Features

White, grey and black plumage, with long tail which is repeatedly wagged.

Secondary Features

White face, dark crown, nape and bib, grey back, white underparts, and black tail with white outer feathers. European White Wagtail **(1)** is replaced in Britain by the black-backed (male only) subspecies **(2)**.

Localities, Habitats and Song

Inhabits any open country in which insects can be found. Undulating flight becomes rapidly erratic when chasing insects on the wing. On the ground, intersperses dashes after insects with pauses to wag tail.

Lookalikes and Their Features

(**Pied Flycatcher:** much shorter tail; very upright posture.)

Dipper

18 cm Resident **7 in**

Primary Features

Stocky brown and white bird.

Secondary Features

Although apparently uniformly brown, head and belly are chestnut and the remainder is brown-black. Breast and throat are pure white.

Localities, Habitats and Song

Always near fast-flowing streams and rivers. Catches insects above and below the water surface. Walks along stream bed against current using wings to hold it down. Defends a stretch of stream against all-comers. 'Curtseys' repeatedly.

Lookalikes and Their Features

None.

Swallow

19 cm Summer Visitor **7¹/₂ in**

Primary Features

Long forked tail and red face.

Secondary Features

Blue-black back and pinkish underparts. Blue band across throat and blue cheeks border the red face. The tail feathers have white spots above and patches below.

Localities, Habitats and Song

Acrobatic flier, twisting and turning to catch insects often at very low level. Frequently nests inside farm buildings.

Lookalikes and Their Features

House Martin: white rump.

Sand Martin: brown breast-bar; white underparts.

Swift: scythe-like wings; uniform brown plumage.

Common Sandpiper

19 cm Summer Visitor **7¹/₂ in**

Primary Features

Light brown 'saddle' mark across neck.

Secondary Features

Soft brown upper parts unusual for a wader. Pure white underparts and a streaked breast. In flight, shows conspicuous white wing-bars, and the white rump and outer tail feathers are divided by brown.

Localities, Habitats and Song

Low flight; stiff, bowed wings; and shallow rapid wing-beats are unique amongst waders, as is bobbing of tail like a Wagtail. Call is a clear 'twee-see-see'. Anywhere near water in summer; in autumn and winter on coasts and estuaries.

Lookalikes and Their Features

(Wood Sandpiper: lacks dark centre to tail; lacks wing-bar.)

(Green Sandpiper: very dark back; white rump; lacks wing-bar.)

Redwing

20 cm Winter Visitor **8 in**

Primary Features

Bright red flanks and underwing.

Secondary Features

Typical Thrush with speckled breast. Prominent white stripe over eye is often most easily seen feature.

Localities, Habitats and Song

Gregarious winter visitor to open areas and larger gardens seeking berries and fruit, worms and insects. Often flocks with Fieldfares.

Lookalikes and Their Features

Song Thrush: lacks eye-stripe; orange underwing.

Mistle Thrush: larger; lacks eye-stripe; white underwing; white outer tail feathers.

Fieldfare: grey head; brown back; grey rump; white underwing.

Fieldfare

25 cm Winter Visitor **10 in**

Primary Features

Grey head, brown back and grey rump.

Secondary Features

A large thrush with typical speckled breast. Black tail, white underwing and golden throat and upper breast. Dark brown upper wing.

Localities, Habitats and Song

Extremely gregarious, often flocking with Redwings. Frequents the middle of fields, especially if damp.

Lookalikes and Their Features

Mistle Thrush: brown crown, back and rump.

Song Thrush: smaller; orange underwing.

Redwing: red underwing; prominent eye-stripe.

Snipe

27 cm Resident **10¹/₂ in**

Primary Features

Zig-zag flight and 'scaap' alarm-call when flushed.

Secondary Features

Rich brown back streaked with buff and black. White belly. Breast and flanks buff with dark markings. Crown black with buff streak. Tail rich brown barred with black. Long, straight bill roughly one quarter of the body-length.

Localities, Habitats and Song

Inhabits most wet habitats from bogs to salt marshes. Well camouflaged and secretive, usually seen only when flushed. In spring, conspicuous display flight in which bird dives through air, vibrating tail feathers making 'drumming' sound.

Lookalikes and Their Features

(**Jack Snipe:** similar; smaller; flushes silently with shorter, more direct flight.)

(**Woodcock:** larger; not gregarious; inhabits woodland.)

As shown here, the Snipe is well camouflaged which means he is only seen when flushed out.

Little Grebe (or Dabchick)

27 cm Resident **10¹/₂ in**

Primary Features

Small size and distinctive shape, and (in summer) yellowish base to bill.

Secondary Features

Summer: dark brown with chestnut cheeks and throat. Tail is blunt-ended and often fluffed. Winter: plumage paler; chestnut turns to buff; flanks fade to buff.

Localities, Habitats and Song

Inhabits any stretch of quiet water. Though common, habits are skulking and may be difficult to see for any length of time. Dives frequently.

Lookalikes and Their Features

(Black-Necked Grebe: summer – drooping golden ear tufts; winter – black and grey neck; upturned bill.)

Sparrowhawk

28–38 cm Resident **11–15 in**

Primary Features

Broad, round-tipped wings and barred underparts.

Secondary Features

Male has blue-grey upper parts, brick-red underparts. Smaller (28 cm/11 in) than female (38 cm/15 in). Female has brown upper parts with strongly barred tail. Pale underparts. White eyebrow. Both sexes have yellow legs.

Localities, Habitats and Song

Always close to woodland preferring mixed country with woods and open farmland. Small birds and sometimes mammals taken from swift, low flight, usually shooting out from behind cover of a hedge, etc. Soars but does not hover.

Lookalikes and Their Features

Buzzards (and **Eagle**): much larger; short tails.

Kestrel (and all **Falcons**): pointed wings.

Kestrels: hover.

(**Harriers:** long narrow wings.)

(**Kites:** forked tails.)

♂

♀

The Sparrowhawk soars but does not hover, taking small birds and using swift, low flight.

Partridge

30 cm Resident **12 in**

Primary Features

Orange-red face and pale grey neck and breast.

Secondary Features

Typical game bird. Has round, chicken-like shape. The back, upper wing, rump and inner tail are all brown with buff streaks. Outer tail and horseshoe-shape patch on belly are chestnut. Flanks barred chestnut. Underparts pale grey.

Localities, Habitats and Song

Very shy bird usually seen in small flocks (coveys) on cultivated land and occasionally on heaths and moors. Takes flight on whirring wings at the least disturbance. Lays enormous clutches, up to 20 eggs, in hedgerows.

Lookalikes and Their Features

Red-Legged Partridge: similar at a distance; white face; black 'necklace'.

Red Grouse: entirely red-brown.

Lapwing

30 cm Resident **12 in**

Primary Features

Long crest and laboured flapping flight on broad, round-tipped wings.

Secondary Features

Though appears black and white at a distance, is actually mainly dark green and white.

Orange under the tail.

Localities, Habitats and Song

Eerie 'peewit' call gives bird its country name. Calls often from tumbling display flight. Flocks in winter on farmland and other open ground. A member of the Plover family. Like other waders favours marshy land, especially when breeding.

Lookalikes and Their Features

None.

Moorhen

33 cm Resident **13 in**

Primary Features

White stripe on flank.

Secondary Features

Though often appearing black, plumage is dark brown. Red shield above bill and white outer tail feathers also very distinctive.

Localities, Habitats and Song

Favours variety of fresh water habitats from small ponds to large reservoirs. Easily disturbed, displays alarm by flicking tail to display white outer feathers.

Lookalikes and Their Features

Coot: white shield above; lacks stripes on flank.

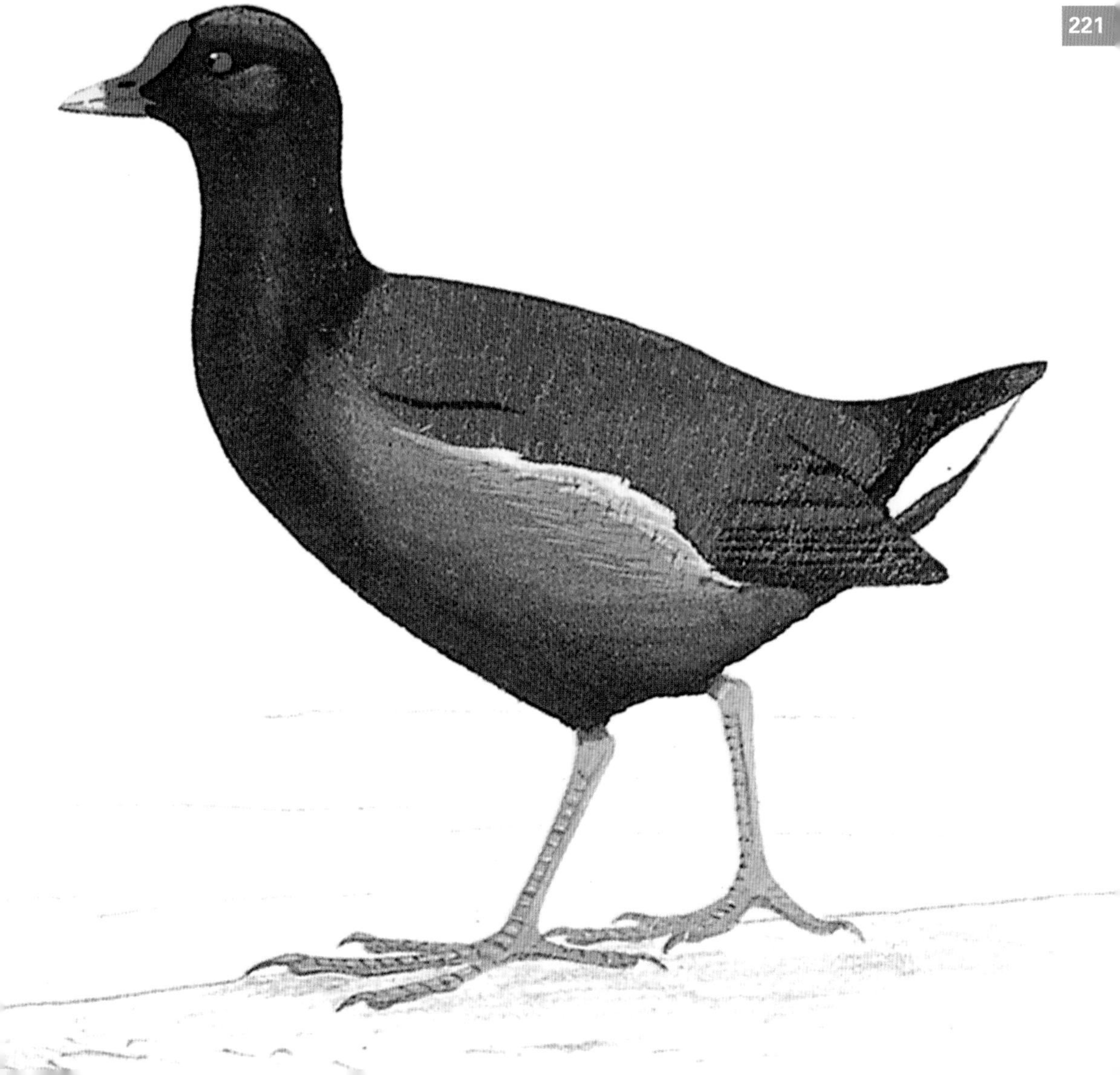

When alarmed the Moorhen flicks its tail to display its bright white outer feathers.

Stock Dove

33 cm Resident **13 in**

Primary Features

Upper wing has black borders, lower wing does not.

Secondary Features

Lacks any white markings. Plumage generally drab grey, but for black tip to tail, green patch on neck and pink breast.

Localities, Habitats and Song

Inhabits woods and open country. Flight is fast and direct. Often flocks on farmland.

Lookalikes and Their Features

Feral Pigeon: usually lacks pink breast; black border below wing, not above.

Wood Pigeon: white flashes on wing.

Collared Dove: zig-zag black collar.

(Turtle Dove: pied markings on neck.)

Kestrel

33–36 cm Resident **13–14 in**

Primary Features

Hovers for long periods.

Secondary Features

Pointed wings and long thin tail of a Falcon. Male has blue-grey head, rump and tail. Back and inner wing rufous, with black spots. Outer wing and tail tip black. Female has upper parts rufous, barred with black. Tail tip black.

Localities, Habitats and Song

Widely distributed in all types of country. Has successfully adapted to towns and particularly to motorway verges.

Lookalikes and Their Features

All **Hawks:** broad, round-tipped wings.

Buzzard (and **Eagle**): much larger.

(**Harriers:** much larger.)

(**Kites:** forked tails.)

(Other **Falcons** do not hover.)

♀

♂

Having successfully adapted to towns, Kestrels are now often spotted close to motorway verges.

Red-Legged Partridge

34 cm Resident **13¹/₂ in**

Primary Features

Black band passing through eye and around neck.

Secondary Features

Typical game bird with plump, chicken-like shape. White face. Upper parts plain brown and outer tail chestnut. Buff belly. Breast and most of underwing grey. Flanks barred black, white and deep red. Legs and bill red.

Localities, Habitats and Song

Like Partridge, generally in small flocks (coveys) on agricultural land, but also on heaths and even coastal dunes. Very wary, will run off rather than fly. Lays up to 16 eggs in nest hollow scraped under cover.

Lookalikes and Their Features

Partridge: similar at a distance; orange face; grey neck; no black stripe on grey neck; horseshoe on belly.

Red Grouse: entirely red-brown.

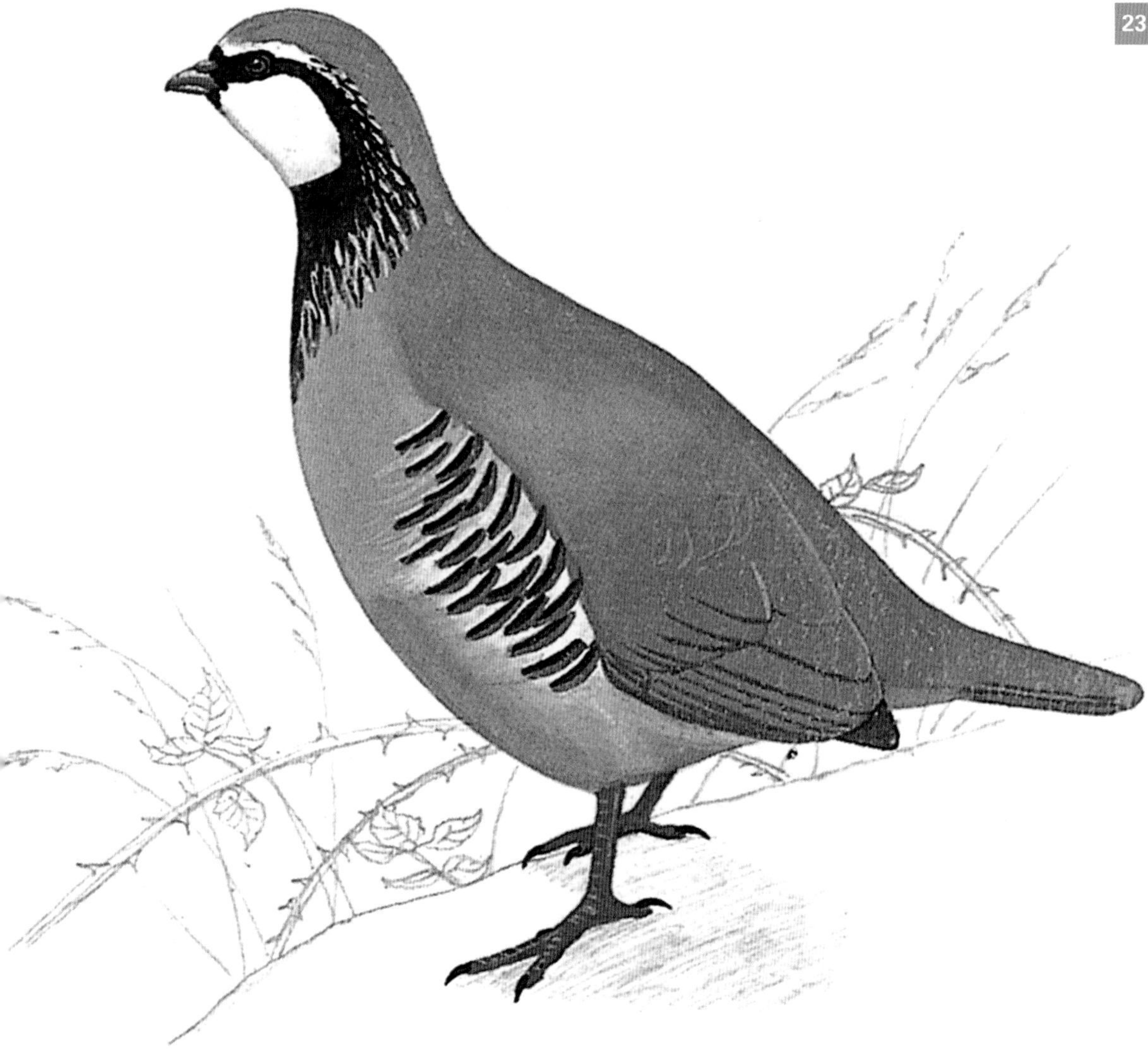

A shy and very wary bird, the Red-Legged Partridge is generally found in small flocks.

Barn Owl

34 cm Resident **13¹/₂ in**

Primary Features

Owl with unmarked, white underparts.

Secondary Features

Beautiful orange and buff mottled upper parts contrasting with white, heart-shaped face.

Localities, Habitats and Song

Often nests and roosts in rural buildings. Otherwise favours woodland and marshy places. Mainly nocturnal, most often seen at twilight. Flight is buoyant and unhurried, with periodic short glides.

Lookalikes and Their Features

All other **Owls:** dark or streaked underparts.

Shown here in flight, the Barn Owl has a beautiful orange tint to its mottled upper half.

Willow and Red Grouse

33–39 cm Resident **13–15$^{1}/_{2}$ in**

Primary Features

Chicken-shaped moorland bird with white-feathered feet.

Secondary Features

Colour varies from all-white plumage of Willow Grouse **(1)**, through white and red-brown summer plumage to the fully red-brown Red Grouse **(2)**. Males show a red wattle above the eye.

Localities, Habitats and Song

Restricted to Northern Europe, except for infrequent visitors, these species favour heather moorland, lowland heaths and bogs. Flight is strong and low, swift wingbeats alternating with long glides.

Lookalikes and Their Features

Partridge: orange-red face; grey neck.

Red-Legged Partridge: white face; black stripe across chest.

Teal

35 cm Resident **14 in**

Primary Features

Smallest duck with green and black speculum; white wing-bars, prominent before speculum, obscure behind.

Secondary Features

Male has chestnut head. Green patch around eye. Grey back, wings and flanks. Spotted, buff breast. Yellow triangle under tail. At rest, horizontal white stripe above wing. Female is buff-brown. Underparts paler and heavily spotted.

Localities, Habitats and Song

Fast fliers on rapid wing-beats, often in large flocks which twist and turn in flight. Favour wet, marshy areas in the breeding season, and reservoirs, lakes and sewage farms at other times.

Lookalikes and Their Features

None.

The male Teal is easily identified because of the green patch around its eye.

Coot

38 cm Resident **15 in**

Primary Features

White shield over bill.

Secondary Features

Entirely black except for greenish legs and lobe-webbed feet.

Localities, Habitats and Song

More aquatic than the Moorhen, Coots favour wide stretches of open water. Gregarious birds, they often flock in winter on lakes and gravel pits.

Lookalikes and Their Features

Moorhen: white stripes on flank; red shield above bill.

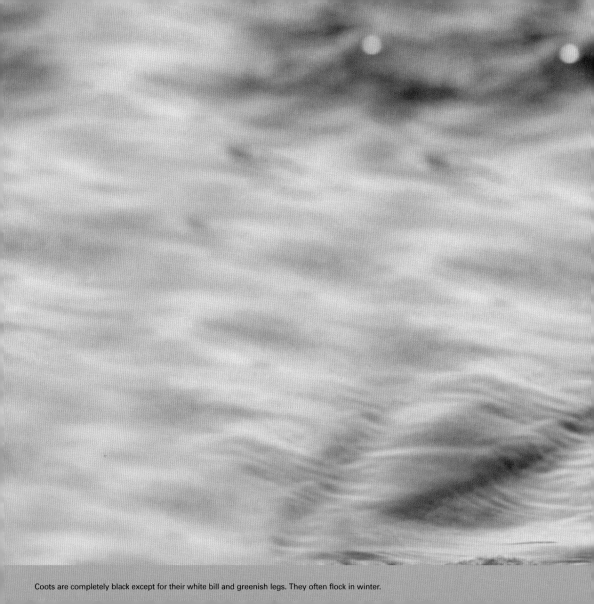

Coots are completely black except for their white bill and greenish legs. They often flock in winter.

Tufted Duck

43 cm Resident **17 in**

Primary Features

The only duck with a crest (more prominent in male).

Secondary Features

Male is all black except for pure white flanks. Female plumage is duller but reminiscent of male, occasionally with small white mark at base of bill. Both sexes have white wing-bar, prominent when in flight.

Localities, Habitats and Song

Numerous freshwater diving duck. Often flocks with other ducks in winter on ponds, reservoirs, etc.

Lookalikes and Their Features

None

Pochard

46 cm Resident **18 in**

Primary Features

Male has chestnut head, black breast and bluish band around bill. Female markings are reminiscent of male but duller. Bluish band around bill.

Secondary Features

Remainder of bill black. Lack of distinct wing markings (nondescript grey bar only). (Male) light grey back and flanks, black rump and under-tail. (Female) brown but reminiscent of male. Buff band around the cheeks.

Localities, Habitats and Song

Inhabits slow-moving waterways, preferring lakes, reservoirs, etc. A diving duck which runs across the water when taking off.

Lookalikes and Their Features

(**Wigeon:** buff crown; lacks black breast.)

Other female **Ducks:** lack black bill with blue band.

Rook

46 cm Resident **18 in**

Primary Features

Entirely black with pale grey face.

Secondary Features

Pale face distinguishes the Rook from the Carrion Crow (except in immatures). Other features include more slender bill, more upright stance, shaggy thigh feathers and wedge-shaped tail in flight.

Localities, Habitats and Song

Normally inhabits agricultural land but also moorland and other open country. Nests in large colonies called rookeries.

Lookalikes and Their Features

Carrion Crow: black face; 'carr' call-note.

Jackdaw: grey nape; smaller.

(Raven: huge; 'pruk' call-note.)

As demonstrated here, a defining feature of the Rook is its upright stance. It nests in large colonies called rookeries.

Great-Crested Grebe

48 cm Resident **19 in**

Primary Features

White neck and black ear tufts (tufts small in winter).

Secondary Features

Long pointed bill, long neck, grey back and virtually no tail. Summer: chestnut frills develop below and behind cheeks. Ear tufts enlarge. Winter: no frills, tufts smaller and bill noticeably pinkish.

Localities, Habitats and Song

Inhabits large areas of water such as reservoirs, gravel pits, and lakes. Builds nest in vegetation at water's edge.

Lookalikes and Their Features

None.

Shoveler

51 cm Resident **20 in**

Primary Features

Distinctive spatulate bill. Pale blue forewing and green speculum with white wing-bar.

Secondary Features

Male has green head, white breast, scapulars (outer back) and tip of tail. Chestnut flanks and belly. Centre of back dark brown. Black rump and under-tail. Female is a uniformly mottled brown.

Localities, Habitats and Song

Feeds by dabbling, swimming rapidly with head held low filtering plant food from water surface. When disturbed, rises vertically from the water.

Lookalikes and Their Features

Shelduck: chestnut band across chest; normal bill shape.

All other Ducks: lack spatulate bill.

♀

♂

A pair of Shovelers. These ducks have long, flat 'spatulate' bills and are speedy swimmers.

Buzzard

51–56 cm Resident **20–22 in**

Primary Features

Brown tail with narrow bars.

Secondary Features

Soars effortlessly on straight wings. Tail broad and rounded when fanned. Neck very short. Wing-tips rounded with finger-like tips. Brown back, paler below, streaked.

Localities, Habitats and Song

Frequents secluded areas in hill country and moorland in western England, Wales and Scotland. May perch on telegraph poles, fences and so on.

Lookalikes and Their Features

(**Golden Eagle:** neck and head project further; larger – 30–34 in/76–86 cm; north Scotland only.)

(**Rough-Legged Buzzard:** white tail with black band at tip; migratory through north Scotland, east coast of England.)

(**Honey Buzzard:** brown tail with black tip; summer visitor.)

Using their straight wings with rounded tips, Buzzards are able to soar effortlessly. This bird has a very short neck.

Pheasant

53–89 cm Resident **21–35 in**

Primary Features

Extremely long tail.

Secondary Features

Male has green head with red wattled face. White collar. Golden-brown body, breast and flanks with black crescent markings. Female is uniform buff-brown, paler below. In both sexes plumage is variable. Long tail is barred.

Localities, Habitats and Song

Commonest on cultivated farmland, also in woods and open country.

Lookalikes and Their Features

None.

A male Pheasant. The female of the species is buff-brown and has paler underparts.

Mallard

58 cm Resident **23 in**

Primary Features

Purple speculum (band of colour on inner wing), bordered with white.

Secondary Features

Male has yellow bill, glossy green head and upper neck. White collar, brown breast, grey-brown back and wings. Distinctive curly tail feathers. Female has brown bill. All plumage except speculum is a mixture of browns, buffs and black.

Localities, Habitats and Song

Commonest duck in Europe. Surface-feeding on any slow moving water body. Much domesticated, numerous varieties include the pure white Aylesbury. When bred with the wild Mallard mixed offspring are produced.

Lookalikes and Their Features

(Red-Breasted Merganser: white speculum; crest.)

Shoveler: distinctive spatulate bill.

All other **Ducks:** lack purple speculum.

The Mallard is the commonest duck in Europe, but many different varieties exist including the pure white Aylesbury.

Grey Heron

90 cm Resident **35 in**

Primary Features

Grey wings and back.

Secondary Features

Long bill, neck and legs. Black eye-stripe runs into black crest. Black-tipped wings.

Flies with even, leisurely wing-beats, neck folded back between shoulders and legs trailing.

Localities, Habitats and Song

Always near water whether ditches, ponds, rivers or lakes, where it stands motionless waiting to lunge at passing fish. Widespread.

Lookalikes and Their Features

None.

The Grey Heron never strays far from water, be it ditches, ponds, rivers or lakes.

Canada Goose

92–102 cm Resident **36–40 in**

Primary Features

Goose with white patch on face and brown back.

Secondary Features

Black head and neck. Brown wings and belly. White breast and rump. Black tail.

Localities, Habitats and Song

An introduced bird, widely distributed though still low in numbers. Its distinctive markings and liking for small ponds make it a familiar sight. In winter they may gather in large numbers to graze on grassland and marshes.

Lookalikes and Their Features

(**Barnacle Goose:** face entirely white; back grey.)

(**Brent Goose:** far smaller; head dark; white patch halfway down neck.)

(Other **Geese:** lack white on face.)

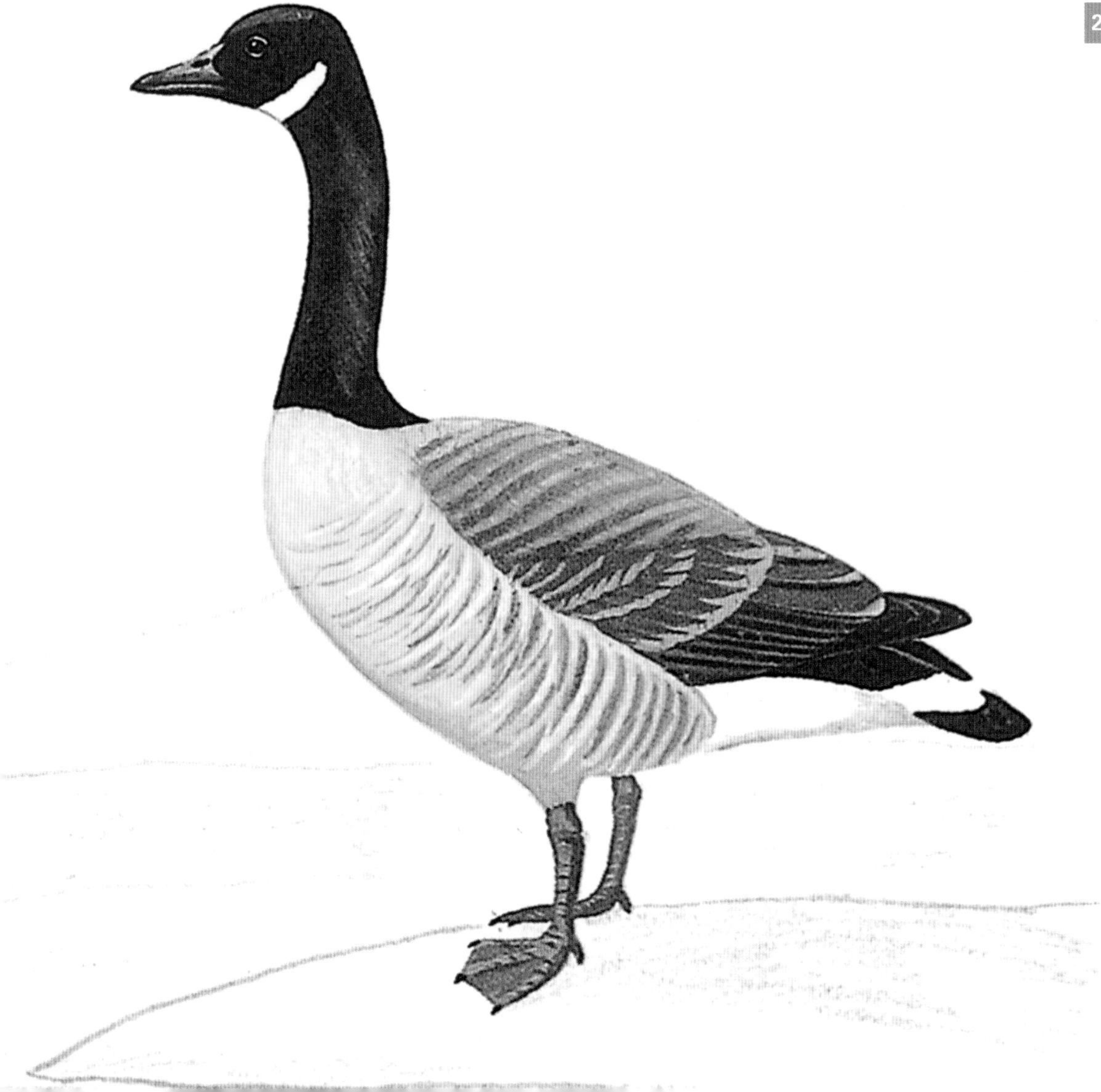

Mute Swan

152 cm Resident **60 in**

Primary Features

Huge white bird with an orange-red bill.

Secondary Features

Distinctive black knob at base of bill, larger in male. Black legs. Body, excluding neck, is about 76 cm (30 in).

Localities, Habitats and Song

Common on slow moving, open water. Graceful S-shape of neck contrasts with other, rarer swans. In flight, noisy throbbing wing-beats may be heard over long distances.

Lookalikes and Their Features

(Bewick's Swan: black and yellow bill; neck held more vertical.)

A pair of Mute Swans transport their chicks. Huge birds, their bodies can be up to 76 cm long.

Rock Pipit

17 cm Resident **6¹/₂ in**

Primary Features

Similar to small Thrush. Grey outer tail feathers. Occurs only on rocky coastlines.

Secondary Features

Dark brown with darker streaks above. Paler breast with dark streaks. Very dark legs.

Localities, Habitats and Song

Inhabits rocky coastlines seeking insects on exposed seaweed. Water Pipits are a different race of this species – much less common, they prefer mountain slope habitats.

Lookalikes and Their Features

Meadow Pipit: paler; white outer tail feathers; pale legs.

(Tree Pipit: yellower breast; 'teeze' call.)

Skylark: bulkier; crest on head.

Dunlin

17–19 cm Resident **7–7$^{1}/_{2}$ in**

Primary Features

In summer, black belly and longish, slightly downcurved bill. In winter, grey-brown back and longish, slightly downcurved bill.

Secondary Features

In summer, chestnut-brown upper parts with black markings. In winter, grey-brown upper parts. Pale grey breast streaks on otherwise white underparts. At all times, in flight, clear wing-bar and white rump divided by black.

Localities, Habitats and Song

Britain's commonest wader. Its striking mannerisms include a 'stitching' feeding motion as it probes the mud. Rather round-shouldered in appearance. Highly gregarious.

Lookalikes and Their Features

(**Golden Plover** and **Grey Plover:** (summer) black belly extends to face; short straight bill.)

(**Sanderling:** (summer): no black belly; short straight bill.)

Knot: (summer): lacks black belly; larger; stockier; straight bill.

(**Little Stint:** tiny; V-mark on back.)

Ringed Plover

19 cm Resident **7¹/₂ in**

Primary Features

Black collar beneath white face with black eye-stripe and band on forehead.

Secondary Features

Small, stout bird, brown above and white below. In flight, conspicuous white wing-bar on upper wing and brown back extends to divide rump. Orange-yellow legs. Bill orange at base and black at tip.

Localities, Habitats and Song

One of Britain's commonest waders, feeding along shore-line on coasts and estuaries. Flight is low and rapid. Often associates with Dunlin.

Lookalikes and Their Features

(**Little Ringed Plover:** lacks white wing-bar; extra line on crown.)

Turnstone: different face pattern; white tail and rump in flight.

Turnstone

23 cm Winter Visitor **9 in**

Primary Features

'Tortoiseshell' back plumage and a dark breastband.

Secondary Features

Upper parts darken in winter to a mottled brown. A plump little bird with bright orange legs and short bill. In flight, entire back and wings distinctively pied.

Localities, Habitats and Song

Entirely coastal, feeding on or around seashores and rocks. Jerky actions and short skittering runs.

Lookalikes and Their Features

Knot (and **Sanderling** and **Purple Sandpiper**) (winter only) lack distinct breast band.

Ringed Plover: black collar beneath white face with black eye-stripe and band on forehead.

Knot

25 cm *Winter Visitor **10 in**

Primary Features

Extremely gregarious. Stout, short-legged wader with scaly grey markings on back. In summer has brown head and underparts.

Secondary Features

Larger and stockier than Dunlin. Grey back and white underparts with grey marked flanks and breast. Pale wing-bar visible in flight, as is pale rump and tail. Bill is straight and short.

Localities, Habitats and Song

Mainly coastal and on estuaries feeding in enormous flocks. Call-note is 'nut' and flight-call 'twit-it'. *Also a passage migrant.

Lookalikes and Their Features

(**Grey Plover:** (summer) black underparts; (winter) black 'armpits'.)

Dunlin: smaller; decurved bill; white rump divided with black.

(**Sanderling:** smaller; dark-legged; very white belly.)

Turnstone: (winter only) distinct breast band.

Redshank

28 cm Resident **11 in**

Primary Features

In flight, white rump and strips on trailing edge of wings form characteristic triple pattern.

Secondary Features

One of Britain's commonest waders. Orange-red legs. Orange-red bill, tipped with black. Brown back. Pale underparts, breast and head all streaked with brown.

Localities, Habitats and Song

Very nervous bird, easily disturbed. Flies off after a couple of dips of the head and a penetrating 'tleu-hu-hu' alarm call.

Lookalikes and Their Features

(**Greenshank:** no white on wings in flight; greenish legs.)

(**Spotted Redshank:** no white on wings; confusion only likely in winter plumage.)

(**Ruff:** faint wing-bar; white rump divided; shorter bill.)

Oystercatcher: pied plumage, though larger white areas on wings and rump similar.

Puffin

31 cm Resident **12 in**

Primary Features

Extraordinary triangular bill, multi-coloured in summer.

Secondary Features

Black crown, nape, back and wings. White underparts, off-white face and bright orange feet.

Localities, Habitats and Song

Extremely fast, 'whirring' wing-beats and splayed feet on landing typical of all auks. Nests in burrows on cliff faces and tops.

Lookalikes and Their Features

None.

A type of Auk, the Puffin nests on cliff tops and faces. Its large triangular beak becomes multi-coloured in summer.

Common Tern

33–36 cm Summer Visitor **13–14 in**

Primary Features

Red bill with black tip in adult.

Secondary Features

Resembles a slender gull with forked tail and buoyant flight. Cap only is black. Grey above and white below with thin dark strip on leading edge of outer wing. Good light shows transparent panel on inner primaries.

Localities, Habitats and Song

Visits Britain March–November. Catches fish by diving from a hovering position. Occurs coastally and at water bodies inland.

Lookalikes and Their Features

Arctic Tern: blood-red bill; short legs.

(Little Tern: smaller; yellow bill.)

(Sandwich Tern: black bill with yellow tip; crest on head.)

Black-Headed Gull: chocolate-brown head (summer).

Arctic Tern

36–38 cm Summer Visitor **14–15 in**

Primary Features

Tern with blood-red bill in adult.

Secondary Features

Resembles a slender gull with forked tail and buoyant flight. Cap only is black. Grey above and white below with white rump. In good light all primaries appear transparent. At rest, noticeably short-legged.

Localities, Habitats and Song

Visits Britain March–September. Catches fish by diving from a hover. Usually coastal.

Lookalikes and Their Features

Common Tern: red bill has black tip.

(**Little Tern:** smaller; yellow bill.)

(**Sandwich Tern:** black bill with yellow tip; crest on head.)

Black-Headed Gull: chocolate-brown head (summer).

Kittiwake

41 cm Resident **16 in**

Primary Features

Black legs and all-black wing-tips.

Secondary Features

White except for grey back and upper wings and black wing-tips. Yellow bill. Juveniles have dark spot on ear, black collar, black 'W' mark on back and wings and black end to tail.

Localities, Habitats and Song

Follows ships with typical buoyant flight. Feeds entirely at sea. 'Kitti-waake' call gives bird its name.

Lookalikes and Their Features

Common Gull: yellow legs; black wing-tips tipped with white.

Black-Headed Gull: red legs; white leading edge to wing; chocolate-brown head in summer.

Razorbill

41 cm Resident **16 in**

Primary Features

Thick black bill marked with white vertical stripe.

Secondary Features

Upper parts and head black. Underparts white. Black feet.

Localities, Habitats and Song

A thick-set auk with typical maritime habits, nesting in cliff-ledge colonies, frequently in association with Guillemots. Flight over sea is low on rapid wing-beats.

Lookalikes and Their Features

Guillemot: sleeker; pointed bill; upper parts very dark brown.

Guillemot

42 cm Resident **16$\frac{1}{2}$ in**

Primary Features

Uniform dark brown upper parts and slender pointed bill.

Secondary Features

Underparts white, feet brown. In winter black cheeks and throat turn white. 'Bridled' form (in limited numbers of the population in any area) has white line around eye and backwards over the ear.

Localities, Habitats and Song

A sleek and slender auk. Thoroughly maritime with low flight on rapidly beating wings. Nests on cliff-ledge colonies, frequently in association with Razorbills.

Lookalikes and Their Features

Razorbill: thick black bill with vertical white stripe.

Oystercatcher

43 cm Resident **17 in**

Primary Features

Pied plumage and long, straight orange-red bill.

Secondary Features

Glossy, black head, throat, back and wings contrast with a white wing-bar, lower breast, belly and rump. Long legs are pink and eyes are red.

Localities, Habitats and Song

A large, common, distinctive wader. Seen singly or in large flocks on seashores, estuaries and other wet areas – sometimes miles inland. A shy bird, it is easily startled into flight giving its shrill piping call.

Lookalikes and Their Features

(**Avocet:** thin upward-curving black bill.)

Redshank: smaller; mainly brown plumage; similar white areas on wings and rump.

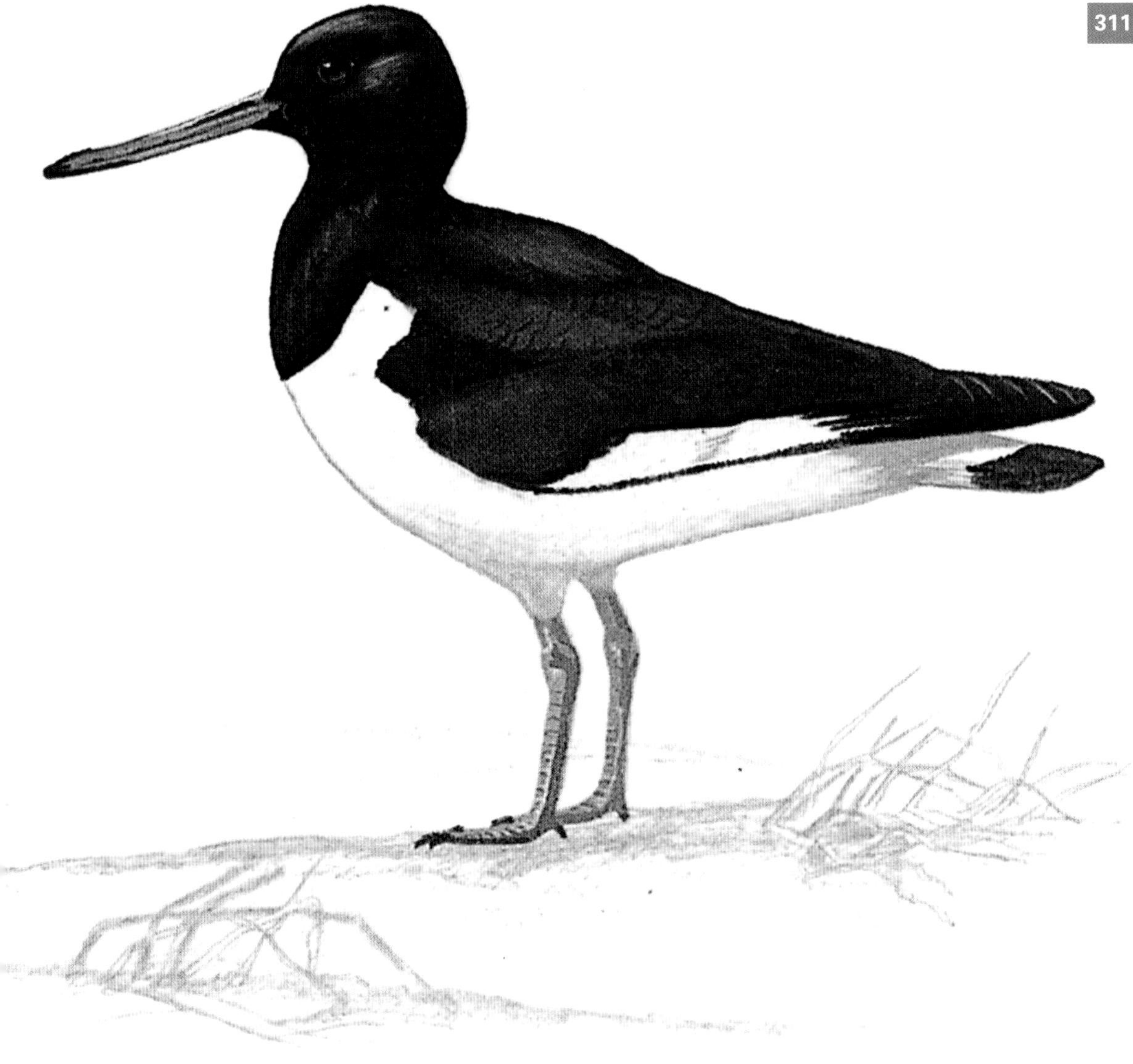

Fulmar

47 cm Resident **18¹/₂ in**

Primary Features

Bull-necked with long wings held straight and stiff in flight.

Secondary Features

Tube-nosed. Grey above, without any black on wings and white below.

Localities, Habitats and Song

Gull-like in appearance but masterful flight quite distinct. Clumsy on land, it has difficulty in landing and taking off. Deters intruders by spitting foul-smelling stomach-oils.

Lookalikes and Their Features

Herring Gull and Common Gull: black tips to wings.

Lesser Black-Backed Gull

53 cm Resident **21 in**

Primary Features

Dark grey back and yellow legs.

Secondary Features

White except for dark grey upper wings. In winter neck is often streaked and legs may fade to grey or even pinkish-grey. Red spot on bill. Juveniles and immatures mottled brown above.

Localities, Habitats and Song

Basically coastal, but may venture inland, especially when migrating, or in winter when resident population widens area of search for food.

Lookalikes and Their Features

Great Black-Backed Gull: very much larger and bulkier; black back; legs always flesh-coloured.

Herring Gull: light grey back and wings; flesh-coloured legs.

Common Gull: smaller and more slender; light grey back and wings; no red bill spot.

The Lesser Black-Backed Gull sometimes ventures inland when migrating but is predominantly a coastal bird.

Curlew

53–58 cm Resident **21–23 in**

Primary Features

Extremely long downward-curved bill. No bold stripes on crown.

Secondary Features

Britain's largest wader. Streaky brown plumage becomes considerably paler towards white belly and rump. Tail is barred brown. Legs are long and grey-green.

Localities, Habitats and Song

Although usually thought of as estuarine, during the breeding season it often inhabits marshy fields and so on. It is gregarious and easily disturbed. Beautiful call is an eerie series of bubbling notes.

Lookalikes and Their Features

None.

Herring Gull

56 cm Resident **22 in**

Primary Features

Grey back and flesh-coloured legs.

Secondary Features

White except for grey upper wings and black wing-ends. Wing-tips are pure white. In winter the neck is streaked. Red spot on bill. Juveniles and immatures are mottled brown above.

Localities, Habitats and Song

Found coastally and inland. A raucous scavenger, frequent at rubbish tips.

Lookalikes and Their Features

Common Gull: smaller and slimmer; yellow legs; no red spot on bill.

Lesser Black-Backed Gull: dark grey back and wings; yellow legs.

Black-Headed Gull (winter only) **:** dark ear-spot; red or deep orange legs; red bill; white leading edge to wings.

Fulmar: straight wings; no black wing-tips.

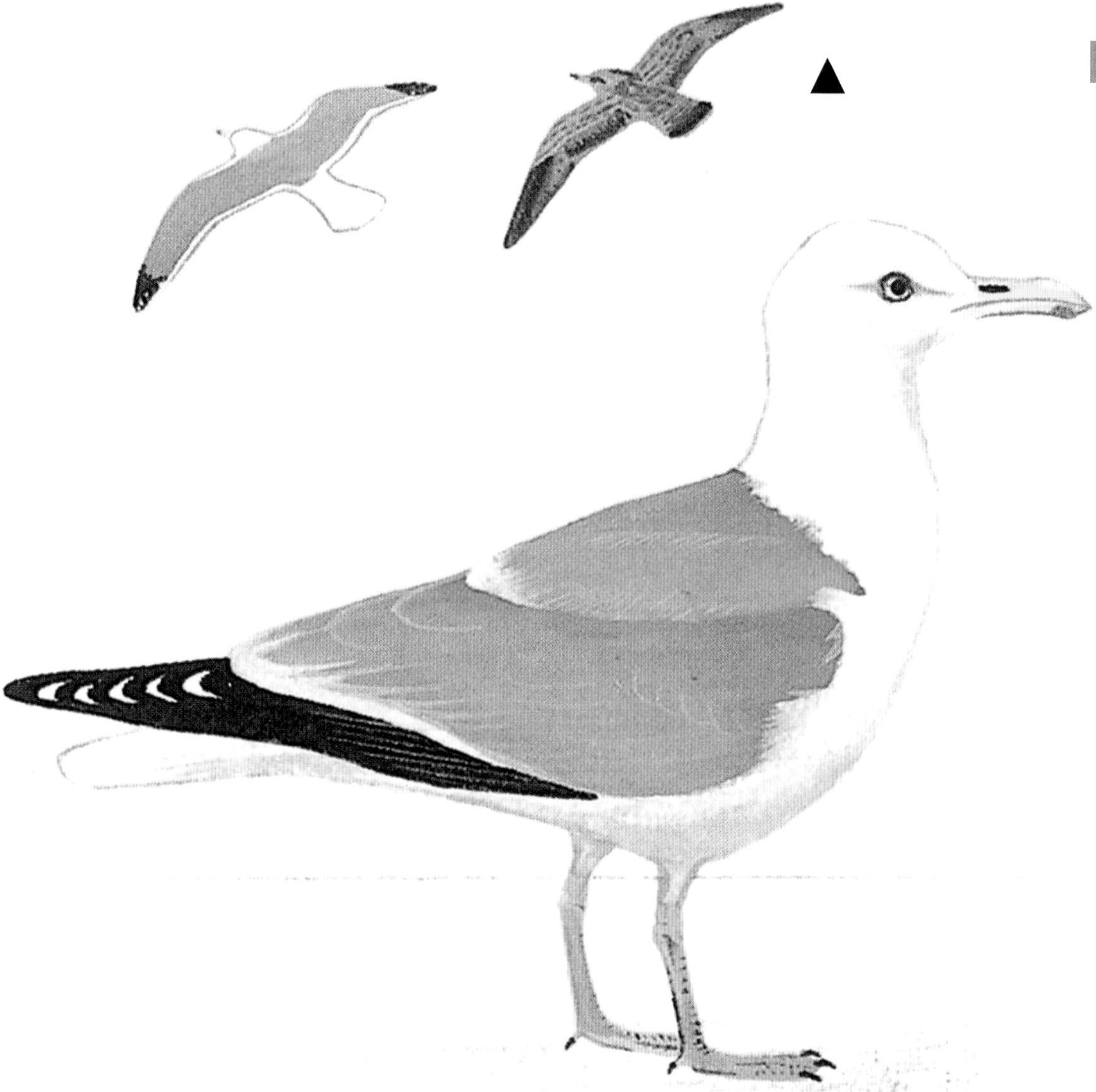

Shelduck

61 cm Resident **24 in**

Primary Features

Black and white with chestnut band around body.

Secondary Features

Large goose-shaped duck with a red bill and pink feet. 'Black' plumage is actually very dark green and wing has a bright green speculum. Bill of male has a red knob.

Localities, Habitats and Song

Estuarine and coastal. General behaviour rather goose-like. Nests in burrows.

Lookalikes and Their Features

Shoveler: extraordinary spatulate bill.

Great Black-Backed Gull

64–69 cm Resident **25–27 in**

Primary Features

Black back and flesh-coloured legs.

Secondary Features

White apart from black upper wing. A very large robust gull with a red spot on bill. Neck may be streaked in winter. Juveniles and immatures are mottled brown above.

Localities, Habitats and Song

Basically coastal, it rarely ventures inland in winter though estuaries are a favourite haunt. May kill small animals and birds as well as being a scavenger.

Lookalikes and Their Features

Lesser Black-Backed Gull: notably smaller and slimmer; dark grey back and wings; yellow legs.

Herring Gull: notably smaller and slimmer, light grey back and wings.

Cormorant

91 cm Resident **36 in**

Primary Features

Black seabird with white cheeks.

Secondary Features

Predominantly blackish all over. White cheeks extend to the chin. White patches on thighs in breeding season.

Localities, Habitats and Song

Almost entirely coastal, it is often seen flying low over the water with a fast direct flight. At rest it perches upright, often with its wings held out to dry.

Lookalikes and Their Features

(**Shag:** bottle-green; crested; lacks white markings.)

Canada Goose: brown wings and back.

The Cormorant flies low over water. As shown here, it rests while perching upright. Its wings are held out to dry.

Gannet

91 cm Resident **36 in**

Primary Features

Massive wingspan approaching 2 m (6 ft).

Secondary Features

The body is distinctly cigar-shaped and the wings long and narrow. Adults have white wings and body, black wing-tips and golden-yellow head. Immatures are speckled black, brown and white in varying degrees.

Localities, Habitats and Song

Flies low over sea in leisurely manner. When feeding on fish performs spectacular dives, often from considerable heights. Wings folded backwards on instant of entry to the water.

Lookalikes and Their Features

None.

Less Common Species

Firecrest 9 cm (3½ in)

Crested Tit 11 cm (4½ in)

♂ ♀

Siskin 11 cm (4½ in)

Little Stint 13 cm (5 in)

Grasshopper Warbler 13 cm (5 in)

Less Common Species

Dartford Warbler 13 cm (5 in)

Wood Warbler 13 cm (5 in)

Pied Flycatcher 13 cm (5 in)

Cetti's Warbler 14 cm (5½ in)

Lesser Whitethroat 14 cm (5½ in)

Less Common Species

Black Redstart 14 cm (5½ in)

Twite 14 cm (5½ in)

Redpoll 14 cm (5½ in)

Little Ringed Plover 15 cm (6 in)

Lesser Spotted Woodpecker 15 cm (6 in)

Less Common Species

Tree Pipit 15 cm (6 in)

Brambling 15 cm (6 in)

Nightingale 17 cm (6½ in)

Bearded Tit 17 cm (6½ in)

Cirl Bunting 17 cm (6½ in)

Less Common Species

Snow Bunting 17 cm (6½ in)

Crossbill 17 cm (6½ in)

Waxwing 18 cm (7 in)

Corn Bunting 18 cm (7 in)

Jack Snipe 19 cm (7½ in)

Less Common Species

Sanderling 20 cm (8 in)

Wood Sandpiper 20 cm (8 in)

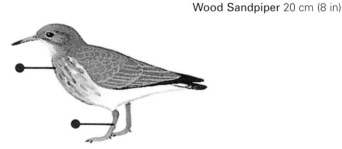

Purple Sandpiper 21 cm (8½ in)

♂ ●
♀ ●

♂ ○

Ruff 22–30 cm (8½–12 in)

Little Owl 22 cm (8½ in)

Less Common Species

Green Sandpiper 23 cm (9 in)

Black Tern 24 cm (9½ in)

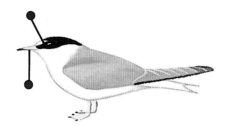

Little Tern 24 cm (9½ in)

Great Grey Shrike 24 cm (9½ in)

Ring Ouzel 24 cm (9½ in)

Less Common Species

Merlin 27–33 cm (10½–13 in)

Turtle Dove 27 cm (10½ in)

Nightjar 27 cm (10½ in)

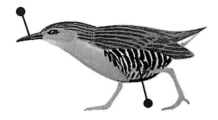

Water Rail 28 cm (11 in)

Golden Plover 28 cm (11 in)

Less Common Species

Grey Plover 28 cm (11 in)

Bee-Eater 28 cm (11 in)

Hoopoe 28 cm (11 in)

Black-Necked Grebe 30 cm (12 in)

Hobby 30–36 cm (12–14 in)

Less Common Species

Spotted Redshank 30 cm (12 in)

Greenshank 31 cm (12 in)

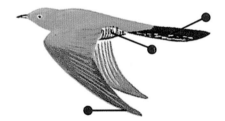

Cuckoo 33 cm (13 in)

Woodcock 34 cm (13½ in)

Manx Shearwater 35 cm (14 in)

Less Common Species

Peregrine 38–48 cm (15–19 in)

Bar-Tailed Godwit 38 cm (15 in)

Short-Eared Owl 38 cm (15 in)

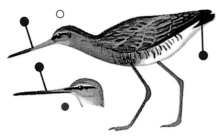

Black-Tailed Godwit 39 cm (15½ in)

Sandwich Tern 41 cm (16 in)

Less Common Species

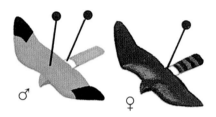

Hen Harrier 43–51 cm (17–20 in)

Avocet 43 cm (17 in)

Wigeon 46 cm (18 in)

Arctic Skua 46 cm (18 in)

Common Scoter 48 cm (19 in)

Less Common Species

Marsh Harrier 48–56 cm (19–22 in)

Gadwall 51 cm (20 in)

Osprey 51–58 cm (20–23 in)

Honey Buzzard 51–58 cm (20–23 in)

Rough-Legged Buzzard 51–56 cm (20–22 in)

Less Common Species

Brent Goose 56–61 cm (22–24 in)

♀

♂

Pintail 55–66 cm (22–26 in)

Barnacle Goose 58–69 cm (23–27 in)

♂

♀

Eider 58 cm (23 in)

♀

♂

Red-Breasted Merganser 58 cm (23 in)

Less Common Species

Great Skua 58 cm (23 in)

Pink-Footed Goose 61–76 cm (24–30 in)

Red Kite 61–64 cm (24–25 in)

Raven 64 cm (25 in)

White-Fronted Goose 66–76 cm (26–30 in)

Less Common Species

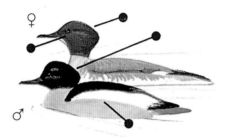

Goosander 66 cm (26 in)

Golden Eagle 75–88 cm (30–35 in)

Grey Lag Goose 76–89 cm (30–35 in)

Shag 76 cm (30 in)

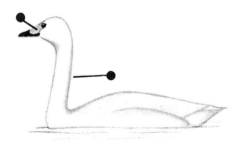

Bewick's Swan 122 cm (48 in)

Further Reading

Burn, H., Holden, P. and Sharrock, J.T.R., *The RSPB Guide to British Birds*, Pan, London, 2002

Campbell, D., *The Encyclopedia of British Birds*, Dempsey Parr, 1999

Cocker, M. and Mabey, R., *Birds Britannica*, Chatto and Windus, 2005

Couzens, D., *Identifying Birds by Behaviour*, Collins, 2005

Couzens, D., *The Secret Lives of Garden Birds*, Christopher Helm Publishers Ltd., 2004

Elphick, J. and Woodward, J., *RSPB Pocket Guide to Birds*, Dorling Kindersley Publishers Ltd., 2003

Golley, M. and Moss, S., *The Complete Garden Bird Book: How to Identify and Attract Birds to Your Garden*, New Holland Publishers Ltd., 2001

Gooders, J., *British Birds*, HarperCollins, 1982

Harrap, S. and Redman, N., *Where to Watch Birds in Britain*, Christopher Helm Publishers Ltd., 2003

Hayman, P. and Hume, R., *The New Birdwatcher's Pocket Guide to Britain and Europe*, Mitchell Beazley, 2002

Hume, R. *RSPB Complete Birds of Britain and Europe*, Dorling Kindersley Publishers Ltd., 2002

Moss, S., *Garden Birds*, Collins, 2004

Perrins, C.M. (ed), *The New Encyclopedia of Birds*, Oxford University Press, 2003

Sterry, P., *Collins British Birds: Photoguide*, Collins, 2004

Sterry, P., *What's That Bird?: Quick Reference Guide to the Most Common European Garden Birds*, Hamlyn, 2006

Svensson, L., and Grant, P.J., *Collins Bird Guide: The Most Complete Guide to the Birds of Britain and Europe*, Collins, 2001

Van den Berg, A., et al, *Birdwatching: The Ultimate Guide to the Birds of Europe*, HarperCollins, 1997

Ward, M., *RSPB Garden Birdwatch*, Dorling Kindersley Publishers Ltd., 2007

Index and Checklist

Keep a record of your sightings by ticking the boxes.